BEGIN WITH CREATIVE WORLD OF CROCHET
BY PAULINE TURNER
CONTENTS

C000298724

FOREWARD

Crochet is perhaps the newest of the traditional textiles. It is a pirate, taking all the ideas and even implements of other crafts in order to produce its own fabrics, fashions, household items and artforms.

It existed as a homecraft long before it became used as a fashion textile or an artform. It is only since the 1970's that various people have begun to explore the potential of the different techniques required in crochet, and make use of the various combinations of stitches, yarns, hooks and colour blendings to create new and exciting effects.

The aim of this series is to look at the recurring problems of crochet and untangle some of the mysteries concerning it that still persist despite the recent introduction of modern and wearable designs which are both figure flattering and comfortable. Similarly the use of crochet in the home no longer relies only on the traditional lace doylies or antimacassars but creates colourful hangings and other articles.

It is hoped that you will be able to teach yourself crochet from this book achieving a sufficiently high standard of finish for you to be able to enter exhibitions and also to achieve whatever award you are looking for, be it the Diploma in Crochet Part I certificate; City and Guilds Creative Studies 790-1-07 competence in crochet certificate; WI certificate, New Zealand Quality Mark - NZSWWS; or any other standard of achievement.

Each chapter covers a different basic process commencing with how to work the particular technique and followed by various methods of experimental suggestions. The information contained encompasses the basic use of a crochet hook. There is also an introduction to hairpin, broomstick, Tunisian and filet crochet.

Each chapter is accompanied by line drawings showing the process, the experimental areas are left to your imagination but outlines suggestions of how to incorporate the ideas into articles.

There are no rules in this book, only guidelines and suggestions to help you discover for yourself the pleasure and satisfaction that crochet can bring at whatever level of competence you achieve or wish to achieve. It is up to you to establish your own rules and once the basic techniques are mastered the door is open to you to exploit the versatility that crochet offers.

Please note this book uses United Kingdom terminology. It is intended that an identical book using United States terminology, yarns and hooks, will be available mid-1992. A conversion chart is given in Appendix I.

CHAPTER ONE
FIRST PRINCIPLES

There are no rigid rules to the crochet in this series, only guidelines that give professional or 'good' rather than hand-made or 'bad' results. Good ways work, bad ways create all manner of complications. Below are various ways of achieving professional results and details of how to overcome the various fallacies that have arisen over the years, creating a great deal of confusion. Please note that NO-ONE should change their way of working if what they do and how they do it produces a good result. Should you have some cause for concern it may be an advantage to try the various ways suggested here to see if there is a way to improve your own crochet fabrics. Otherwise, please ignore this section and start with Chapter 2.

THE HOOK

Most people write, therefore holding a pen or pencil comes fairly easily. If you hold the crochet hook as you would a pencil, you will feel quite comfortable with the implement. Should you be a beginner to the craft it would be wise to choose a conventional wool hook as shown below. Avoid any hook that will bend easily. If you have difficulties with flexing the joints of your hands the plastic handled hooks are warm to hold with the handle being thicker than the stem preventing a need to grip the hook. In fact, with or without manipulation difficulties it is important that you DO NOT grip the hook.

the average hook

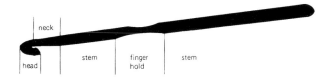

traditional steel or tambour hook

Look at the diagram and see how the neck narrows towards the hook, head away from the stem. It is the STEM that determines the tension of the crochet being worked. All loops placed round the crochet hook should fit the circumference of the stem exactly if a correct tension is to be obtained. Working in the neck of the hook is like working on a smaller size hook simply because the circumference is smaller. Similarly if the loops are very loose and open around the stem of the hook the work will come out larger.

Should you have a selection of old hooks it is quite likely that at least one of the hooks will be shaped like the embroidery tambour hook above. These hooks do not have a straight stem section and unless a finger is placed at exactly the same place throughout the working of the crochet to act as a stop, the work is quite likely to come out unevenly. A beginner to crochet is advised to avoid these types of hooks unless it is intended to only work with very fine cottons the thickness of sewing threads.

Quite a large number of crochet hooks are unmarked. If they have a straight stem, the stem can be inserted into a knitting needle gauge and the size found in precisely the same way as you would a knitting needle. Appendix I is a conversion chart for hooks and is a useful reference for old or foreign patterns as well as comparing different hooks. By the time you have got through the information in this book, there is a strong possibility you will never use a crochet pattern again and the hook you do use will be purely a matter of personal choice!

YARN

Below is a list of points that should be considered when taking the first tentative steps with a new process. Do not let these points inhibit you in any way. Once you are familiar with a technique try it out in ribbon, rope, strips of leather, strips of fabric, string, offcuts from a mill, tied together thrums, or wire, as well as the usual cotton, wool, linen, silk, man-made yarns and all the infinite combinations of any of the fibres that are available in hanks, balls or cones.

a) <u>Aran</u> yarn, whether pure wool or a mixture of wool and man-made fibre, has a crispness that enables it to hold its shape and show the stitch definition off to advantage. This is perhaps the best yarn to use when attempting a new process for the first time.

b) <u>Silky</u> yarns tend to slip and have difficulty holding their form. In addition, the ends of the yarn have a tendency to come undone unless they have been secured more firmly than other yarns.

c) <u>Hairy</u> yarns can hide the stitch structure and are difficult to pull back because of the way the hairs lock into each other. This can be discouraging if you are learning a new process and such a yarn is better avoided until you are familiar with the stitch structure required. It can also result in yarn loss if there is too much pulling back. It is often useful to **face** the light when working with very textured yarns as the light will shine through the holes indicating where to insert the hook.

d) <u>Fine</u> yarns are not the best ones in which to practise a new stitch construction if you have failing eyesight, or if you suffer from stiff fingers. The use of a hook with a plastic handle will help the tension if you have moved from crocheting with a thicker yarn to a fine yarn.

e) <u>Dark</u> colours can be difficult to see in dim or artificial lighting and this can cause eyestrain over a long period of time particularly with tired eyes.

f) <u>Nylon</u> and many other man-made fibre yarns have a tendency to stretch and until you are confident in the way you hold the yarn so that it flows freely through the fingers there is a possibility that the tension will be wrong. The yarn stretches and then after the stitch has been made it will relax causing the stitch to be shorter than the one you thought you worked and creating holes where the yarn should be acting as a filler.

g) <u>Textured</u> yarns such as slubbed, bouclé, chenille, mohair, brushed acrylics and other very textured yarns create an irregular tension to the fabric which is usually included as part of the design feature of the item being made. If you are a beginner, however, trying to get to know the different ways of making crochet fabrics accurately, then it is wise to leave the very textured yarns until you are sure of how the crochet fabric is being produced in the first place. [See 'hairy' yarns]

Crochet is ideal for using all types of unusual fabrics and for being combined with just about every other type of craft so please do not let the comments above deter you from experimenting with everything in sight. The reason for the suggestions above are to help you pass or win whatever award you are seeking to obtain.

HOLDING THE WORK

Find a way to hold the yarn so that if flows easily and with an even tautness through the fingers without causing the arm or fingers to ache. It has been the norm to wrap the yarn round just the little finger, but many people feel that the yarn is then falling off the hand and so grip the little finger tightly into the palm which creates aches and pains up through the finger, arm and elbow, and even reaches the neck. The yarn should flow and the fingers held in a relaxed position as though you were typing or playing the piano.

One solution to the above is to wrap the yarn over two fingers instead of one as shown below, as the fingers can be relaxed and the yarn flows easily.

one way to hold the yarn
(left-handed people refer
to Appendix II)

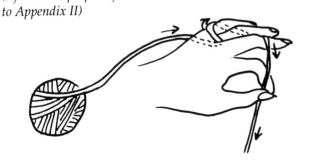

Have the palm of the hand face down, or away from you. Bring the yarn from the palm side to the back of the hand between the middle and ring fingers. Take the yarn over the little and ring finger, then bring it once more from the palm of the hand to the back. This part of the operation creates just sufficient tension on the yarn to keep it taut during the crochet process but without stretching the yarn itself. Finally bring the yarn over the middle and first fingers which can be spread to form a bridge. This allows the hook head to dip easily into the triangle formed by the two fingers and under the yarn, as can be seen in the diagram. The hook then slides under the yarn and catches the thread almost involuntarily. This is the meaning of "yoh, yarn over hook".

If the hook is gripped, this will also create an unwanted tension in the other arm which can reach as far as the spine. Crochet is a therapy and as such the body should always be relaxed and comfortable whilst the fabric is being made.

The actual crochet fabric being made is held and guided by the first finger and the thumb. This sometimes causes difficulties as many people want to put the index finger in the air and hold the fabric with the middle finger and thumb. However, if you could persevere and hold the fabric with the index finger and thumb, you will find that some of the more complex stitches can be worked with greater ease. In particular loop stitches, tambour style surface crochet and many other stitches where it is necessary to feel rather than see where the hook is being guided. Let me reiterate that how you hold the work or the hook should be whatever is comfortable to YOU. There is no right or wrong way to do this. Please do not attempt to change your method of working if it is successful but do try one or two of the suggestions given if you feel that there are areas where you could improve your tension, the finish or wearability of the articles made.

SLIP KNOT

Unless there is a loop on the hook, it is not possible to make a piece of crochet fabric except by tying it into another component   The loop is placed on the hook before any other process is undertaken. Because the loop is actually on the hook before a stitch is commenced, the loop on the hook is NEVER counted as a stitch. No matter how complicated the stitch operation is, it will start and end with a loop on the hook.

Make a slip knot so that there is no yarn wastage when the work is pulled back, because is inevitably pulled back some time. Also try to make a slip knot so that the short end tightens on the hook, as shown below. If you do you will have begun to get into a habit that will stand you in good stead when making buttons, circles for hats or other pieces requiring no hole in the centre. It is also useful for tightening up rectangular pieces of work thus avoiding little lumps at the corner.

a) Wrap the end of the yarn over a circle made from the main ball. Basically you are doing an ordinary slip knot with the main yarn in the left hand and the end of the yarn in the right. [left-handed people please see Appendix II]. Allow the end of the yarn to be approximately 5cm long.

b) Insert the hook under the back thread from right to left and at the same time make sure the hook is lying over both edges of the circle.

c) Hold the main yarn and the end of the yarn and pull the hook up to tighten the loop. Now pull the tail end of the yarn to allow it to hug the circumference of the hook exactly.

HOOK PLACEMENT

Unless your pattern (assuming you are using a pattern) tells you differently, the hook is inserted under two strands of yarn at all times. That is the chain look is picked up at the top of the stitch. The hook is not inserted between the stems of the stitches, as this would be picking up three strands of yarn.

The main exceptions to this rule are :

a) when changing a flat fabric into a textured fabric.

b) when working into the foundation chains. To pick up the chain look with an ordinary crochet hook from the foundation chain is rather clumsy to handle. Have the smooth side of the chain facing and insert the hook towards the bottom of the chain so that there are two threads on the top and one below the stem of the hook as shown below.

c) picking up from the foundation chain for broomstick or Tunisian crochet it is only necessary to pick up one strand rather than two.

working into a chain

Please note that when you are designing your own fab-

rics, it does not matter what you do as long as you do it all the time! Nevertheless, to follow commercial patterns or to write patterns for others to follow, it is essential that two strands are picked up for each stitch unless the instructions state differently.

BREAKING OFF YARN

When a piece of crochet has been completed the yarn has to be broken off. Those familiar with knitting and macrame usually have no problem but many people do not know how to fasten off so that the crochet does not unravel. After the final stitch has been worked, break the yarn away from the main ball leaving approximately 20cm which is sufficient for most finishings. Work one chain and pull the end of the yarn through this chain. Slide the finger and thumb down the yarn to allow the resulting knot to nestle into the work without causing a lump and at the same time preventing the fabric from unravelling.

JOINING YARNS

There are a number of different ways of joining yarn but whichever method is chosen it is important that it is one that cannot be seen, cannot be found quickly by feel, and withstands the wear and tear of general use and laundering.

The following join is simple to make and at the same time is suitable for the majority of non-lacy crochet fabrics. Work the stitch to the point where the old yarn is collected and drawn through to the front of the work, after the hook has been inserted into the row below. Leave this end and finish the stitch with the new ball of yarn. Remove the hook from the stitch (making sure it does not unravel) and you can see that the two ends are now lying on top of the previous row. These can be pulled through the back loop of each stitch for five or six stitches when one of the ends can be cut off. Pull the last strand through a further two or three stitches and fasten off this also. Return to the loop of the stitch and continue working as normal picking up the chain top of each stitch which traps the woven-in strands and keeps them even more securely into place. The only other time this join is unsuccessful is in a firm fabric where the yarn being used is very thick.

joining in new yarn

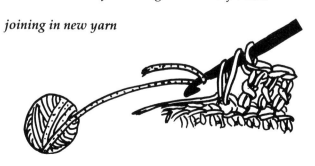

For thick yarns take the precaution of using only one strand of the yarn to loop into the back stitches before working over them. The remaining strand of yarn is dealt with on the next row by pulling it to the top of the stitch and looping into the stitches on that row. This has spread the join, taking one strand one way through the work and the other strand in the opposite direction and on a different level so making the join less noticeable.

If the yarn is extremely slippery to handle such as a viscose or ribbon yarn, it is important that extra precautions are taken to ensure the ends do not unravel during wear and tear. In the case of a ribbon yarn the ends have to be sewn in with a needle and thread [such as polyester] to prevent the ribbon from unravelling on itself and also to stop it from sliding out of the fabric stitch structure. Other rayon yarns can be sewn in using the same method or alternatively a drop of heat and water resistant glue can be put on a pin and inserted down the centre of the stitch(es) where the join and the ends are. Care has to be taken when using glue that the minutest amount is used or the fabric will become stiff and the join is then noticeable. There is one further way in which the ends of slippery yarns can be treated and that is at the design stage where the design allows for the ends of the yarn to come to the right side as a design feature and be part of a tassle or fringe. Do work a join in your tension square where the yarn is difficult, and then launder it, to ensure you have used a suitable technique.

JOINING IN A DIFFERENT COLOUR

The best method of incorporating a new yarn of a different colour is through the last two loops of the stitch being worked prior to the new colour being required. For instance, if the new colour is needed at the start of a new row, the last stitch of the previous row should be worked until there are two loops remaining. The new colour is introduced by completing the last stitch as shown. The hook now has a loop of the new colour on the hook instead of the original making the first chain of the turning chains the new colour. If that process is not carried out, the first chain of the turning chains will be in the old colour and the second chain in the new.

adding a new colour

Designs with more than one colour in the row should ideally be carried and twisted round each other at every stitch or at the most every other stitch to avoid the yarn floating at the back of the work and catching in wear. As with the change of yarn at the end of the row it is necessary to work the stitch before the colour change is required, ie to the point where there are still two loops to be worked in the previous stitch. Finish the stitch with the new colour. It is possible to carry the colour through the stitches from one stitch to another but in most cases the colour will then show through and give a shadow effect to the fabric. Obviously this can work to advantage in a design situation but in most cases it will produce a displeasing effect.

MIXING YARNS AND FIBRES

It is no longer necessary to keep to the same type of yarn throughout the work when making an article. In the past a major drawback to mixing yarns of different fibre content has been the problem of laundering. With the advent of cold water washes it is now possible to mix different fibres as well as different textured yarns, within the same article which gives the crochet worker enormous scope previously unavailable. Follow the instructions given by the manufacturer and all will be well. Do not hesitate to use a washing machine if it is of the kind recommended but DO finish the drying process with the article lying flat.

It is a good idea to protect lacy and other very delicate fabrics by placing them in a white polyester lightweight pillow case or muslin bag. Use top loading washing machines and COLD water placing slightly less than the recommended quantity of Woolite or other product into the water giving a quick swish of the water to mix the solution thoroughly. None-lacy items can be placed directly into the machine along with those in the prepared bags. If the items to go in the machine have long ties that are going to snarl up in the machine, remove them or fasten them so that they cannot wrap round sleeves, collars, etc. In addition take the precaution of fastening up buttons and zips. Obviously do not mix strong colours with whites and creams, but otherwise it is not necessary to take other safeguards.

GETTING A CORRECT TENSION

First work a piece of crochet not less than 10cm square if the yarn is of 3-ply to double knitting thickness, and 15cm square for thicker yarns. Measure only in the centre of the square worked as the first two rows containing the foundation chain should be ignored to allow for the changes that can occur if the foundation chain is not exactly the same tension as the rest of the work. It also allows you to get used to the stitch structure, yarn and hook being used for the item being made. The edges should also be ignored as these can be quite irregular depending upon the yarn, the stitch pattern and the way the work is turned. If the pattern has proved troublesome when doing the tension square, it will pay you to work a second piece and measure the second piece rather than the one where you have been working out how to put the pattern together.

Always smooth the crochet from the <u>base of the stitch to the top.</u> That is away from the foundation chain and not from side to side! Put the tension square to be measured onto a smooth surface so that the threads of the crochet do not cling to other fibres. The surface should also be flat as any curvature will alter the accuracy of the measurements. Then measure the centre portion only.

measuring tension

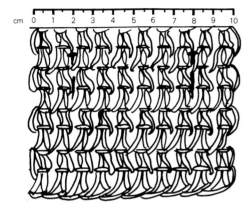

If you are following a pattern you will be given the number of stitches and hopefully the number of rows, to a specified number of centimetres. Check that your tension square is at least 5cm larger than those given both in width and length to ensure an accurate measure. If there are too few stitches the tension is too loose, conversely if there are too many stitches the tension is too tight.

NOTE: if the tension is out by only half a stitch over a 5cm square the finished article will be 10cm too large or too small when there are 5sts to 5cm and the size required is 100cm!

NAMES OF ROWS

Some patterns refer to rows by special names and this can be confusing, especially if you are new to crochet. A 'foundation' row is the row worked into the initial or foundation chain. That is the chain which starts the fabric off in the first place.

The very first row of crochet is frequently different from the rest of the work, for instance, you may start by "work 1tr into the 4th ch from the hook", but on the following row you "work into next st". It is for this reason that patterns are frequently written with a foundation row, and are then followed by a pattern row or sequence of rows. Once the 'foundation' row has been worked it is not used again except when starting another section of the article. **PLEASE NOTE:** Old patterns advocate working a double crochet row before commencing the pattern and in fact treat the foundation chain and one row of double crochet as a natural start to every pattern. This method of working gives added firmness to the base row which is suitable to only 30% of the designs!

A 'pattern' row is the row that will be repeated throughout the work. It is possible there is only one row which is referred to as the pattern row. However, there may be many pattern rows which could be written as "1st patt row, 2nd patt row, 3rd patt row", etc. Normally pattern repeats are given as: "rows 2-7 inclusive form the patt, repeat for length required".

ABBREVIATIONS

Different designers and different countries use different words to describe the same stitch, stitch process, or series of stitches. It is important therefore to **read the abbreviations** given at the front of a pattern or in the index of a book, before starting the crochet. This will avoid all kinds of frustrations. Appendix III has a list of abbreviations for the United Kingdom and the United States as well as the international symbols for each of the commonly used stitches and stitch combinations.

READING A CROCHET PATTERN

Basically the following points are the ones to watch for when reading a commercial pattern. Having worked through the techniques in this book there is a strong probability you will know better ways to achieve an excellence in tension, finish, and yarn usage, than those in the pattern you are following. This is not a derogatory comment on crochet designers but an observation that few designers have been trained or have the analytical know-how in crochet because crochet is such a young textile. Weavers, knitters, and other needlecrafts have been producing information on techniques for a long time. Crochet has not. It is advised you use commercial patterns to obtain the design you require if you do not wish to design one for yourself, but that you incorporate whatever technical improvements you can as you proceed with the working of the article.

1: Read the pattern by working all the information between commas as **one** operation. This should give you the number of stitches you need, the type of stitches you need, and the place where you are to put those stitches.

2: Patterns produced before 1980 are likely to have stitches missed for decreases instead of decreasing two stitches together, therefore change the pattern to avoid steps or holes at the edges.

3: If the suggested hook size is the same as the knitting needle size for the yarn being used, the fabric is likely to be stiff and use far too much yarn, therefore reduce the thickness of yarn being recommended. For instance use a 4-ply instead of a double knitting or a 3-ply instead of a 4-ply. Keep the same size hook as the one recommended for the thicker yarn in the pattern being used.

4: Some patterns put repeats in brackets, for instance (1tr,1ch,miss 1st,1dc)6times. This means everything in the brackets has to be worked 6times in all. Some patterns use asterisks, for instance *1tr, 1ch, miss 1st, 1dc, rep from *5 times. This means everything will be worked 6 times also, once from the asterisk plus 5 more times.

5:      Crochet stitches are different heights which means that the turning chains will be different for rows using different stitches. The turning chains are calculated in the base chains and the number of turning chains at the beginning of a row will collectively count as the first stitch of that row. See the respective sections on the various stitches for the number of turning chains needed for that stitch. Turning chains are necessary to lift the hook to the required height of the next row.

6:      Crochet has no right or wrong side to it unless you make it have a right or a wrong side because of the texture included in it or because of some form of shaping. Some patterns will say at the beginning of the work after only one row has been given "with right side facing". Mark the crochet with a safety pin as the right side after you have turned the work to commence row 2.   There may be a need in the pattern to know that this has become the right side.

7:      Patterns often say "work 4 rows dc for border" without any further help to the crochet worker.   There will be no indication of the number of stitches required for the border to lie flat, or whether or not there should be either increases or decreases to take the border round corners or inside curves. If the same yarn and the same size hook is being used for the borders as in the main fabric, 3dcs to two tr rows will give a flat border. At right angle corners 2dc on one row and 3dc on the next will be needed in the corner stitch, and irregular dc2tog will have to be included in a neck or armhole curve. If the border is continuous it is adviseable to join with a slip stitch and **turn** on every round or the borders will curl up and the look of the border will be quite different to those that are turned on every round.

CHAPTER TWO
CHAIN AND SLIPSTITCH

Abbreviation: ch and ss. ⭕ and ⌢ .
No turning chain needed.

CHAINS

To make a chain, commence with a slip knot on the hook. Place the yarn over the hook (yoh) by dipping the hook head under the strand of yarn lying between the fingers as shown. The yarn will automatically catch in the barbed part of the hook head and can then be drawn through the loop (lp) of the slip knot already on the hook. Do make sure that the smooth part of the hook head is uppermost so that the yarn caught in the barb can slide through the loop on the hook. If the barb is uppermost then it is rather like catching a fish and the new loop cannot be made. However, if the hook is facing directly down, the yarn will not stay in the hook head. The ideal position therefore is to have the hook head facing the shoulder which will prevent the need to twist the hook during the process of making a crochet stitch.

making a chain

One chain has been made. Continue in this manner until a sufficient number of chains have been worked. Do not count the loop on the hook as this is the initial slip knot. All crochet begins and ends with one loop on the hook and therefore the loop is not a stitch.

Chains are used for:

a   Foundation chains. This is a length of chain determined by the number of stitches to be used in the fabric being made.   Each chain represents a stitch after taking away the number of turning chains being used less one.

b   Turning chains. A turning chain is made at the end of each row to lift the crochet hook to the top of the row about to be made. Note the crochet hook 'sits' on top of the row being worked and therefore has to be raised to this level before proceeding with the next row of crochet.

c   Linking chains (not slip stitches). Chains can be used to link pieces of fabric together that have a lacy design, so that the joins are not ugly or too noticeable.

SLIP STITCH

A slip stitch is a chain that is anchored to a stitch. There is no height to a slip stitch. To make a ss, insert the hook into the work picking up 2 strands of yarn unless the pattern tells you differently, yoh, draw up the yarn through the place where the hook is inserted and through the loop already on the hook.

slip stitch

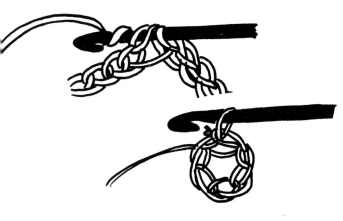

One slip stitch is made. The main uses of slip stitches are:

a   To join rows together to make rounds when working circles for motifs, doilies, hats, etc.

b   To join rows together to make tubes when making seamless sleeves, trouser legs, gloves, etc.

c   To carry the yarn over stitches which no longer need to be worked, for instance at the beginning of a decrease row when more than three stitches are being decreased at a time. By working a ss into each stitch, no extra height has been added to the work and each stitch retains the chain look which is needed for future crochet processes.

d   As a connecting stitch in some crochet fabric patterns.

WORKING A PIECE OF CHAIN AND SLIPSTITCH NET

Now that the hook can be manipulated sufficiently to produce a slip knot, chain and slip stitch, try the following crochet net which can be used for string shopping or beach bags; silk, acrylic, or mohair scarves and stoles; garden nets worked in fine fishing line; net curtains using 10's mercerised cotton; overtops, etc.

Warning! This is not the easy-to-make fabric that it looks. It is **most** difficult to keep the tension exactly right so please do not be discouraged at your first attempts. To work any of the above items, slightly incorrect tensions will not be noticeable but before starting check the fol-

lowing points.

a   Check the tension by making a small piece using the correct hook and the yarn for the article. Besides finding out whether the tension is correct you will also become familiar with the stitch pattern. Work a piece commencing with 29 chain which gives six loops and work at least 12 rows. It is important the chains are not too uneven as they will show. Most beginners have a tendency to crochet chains tightly. Please check the chains are loosely worked.

b   It is usual to pick up two strands of yarn unless the pattern states differently. Note this pattern picks up only one strand on the foundation chain, **two** strands for the very last slip stitch of the row, and under **all the chain** in the middle of the rows.

c   There is no right or wrong side to crochet until you make it have a right or wrong side. In this pattern that means the work is reversible until after the seams are made.

d   Joining in a new ball of yarn is more difficult with an open pattern. To get a neat join in this lacy network, first finish with a slip stitch, make one chain and pull the end through this chain as though completing the work. Insert hook into 5chsp just made, close to the final ss, pull yarn through to right side. Work 1ch with the two threads (that is the tail end and ball thread of the new yarn), work 4ch with the ball thread. Go back to the 2 short ends and tie a reef knot sewing them into the fabric separately at a later stage.

e   Where the pattern says '1ss in ch sp' it means inserting the hook into the hole or loops made by the 5ch of previous row. If pattern says '1ss in next ch', it means inserting the hook into the actual chain stitch.

f   When making any extensions for sleeves, etc with this pattern to give a T-shape, it is important they are both added on the same row at the same time or one extension will be higher than the other causing one sleeve to be narrower than another. This applies to any pattern where chains have to be added on both ends of the same row.

g   The foundation row has to stretch over the upper part of the hips when making a fashion garment worked from base to the neck. If this foundation chain is crocheted too tightly it will not fit comfortably round the body. The only exception to working a loose foundation chain is if the fashion garment is worked from the sleeve downwards. A tighter chain on the shoulders helps the garment to hang better.

h   Counting the rows is easier in this pattern if the diamonds are counted. Multiply by 2 as 2 rows equals one diamond.

i   When putting two pieces together for joining, it is simpler if the 6ch loops made for the beginning of the row are placed together. It is important that the ss made during the joining are worked very loosely indeed or the seams will be tight and give a gathered look rather than the straight line that is being aimed for.

NETWORK PATTERN OF SLIPSTITCH AND CHAIN

Work on a multiple of 4ch plus 5ch to get the correct size. A small trial size could be as follows:

Make 29ch.

Row 1: 1ss in 9th ch from hook [one strand], *5ch,miss 3ch,1ss in next ch, rep from * to end, 6ch, turn. (6loops)
Row 2: *1ss in 5chsp,5ch,rep from * to last sp,1ss in 4th ch,6ch,turn.
Rep row 2 to length required.

If patt requires a straight edge at top of work, make a final row of 2 (or 3)ch and 1ss.

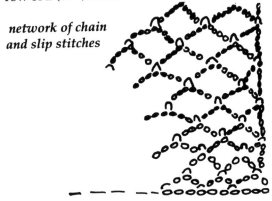

network of chain and slip stitches

EXPERIMENTAL TECHNIQUES using slipstitch and chain

To appreciate the versatility of crochet one has to experiment with various hook sizes and alternative types of yarn. Although the stitch pattern is not altered, the crochet fabric being produced will look and feel quite differently just by changing the size of the hook. The smaller the hook, the firmer the fabric; conversely with a larger hook the crochet fabric will feel softer and be more open. In a similar way the fabric will alter by changing the type and thickness of the yarn even though the stitch pattern and hook size remain the same. Therefore a thicker yarn will create a stiffer crochet fabric and a thinner yarn will create a looser and more pliable fabric. The only way to understand how yarns, hooks and stitch patterns react one with another, is to try for yourself. Initially try three hook sizes such as 2.50mm, 5.00mm, and 10.00mm. Use each of these three hooks to make a chain of 30-40 stitches in each of the following five types of yarn:

a   20's crochet cotton
b   a plain smooth acrylic double knitting yarn
c   pure wool of an Aran thickness
d   a thin fluffy yarn such as a 4-ply mohair mixture
e   a thick bouclé or slub yarn

There may be a difficulty initially in keeping a standard tension. One way to overcome the problem is to hold the hook closer to the barbed head when working with fine steel cotton hooks, (0.60-2.00mm) and to hold the very large hooks as far away from the hook head as possible, to the point where most of the hook is between the yarn being worked and the fingers (7.00-15.00mm). This enables the loops to be pushed well down past the tapering section of the hook which leads into the barbed section and so ensures the loops are made to the correct circumference and sit snugly round the stem.

CHAPTER THREE
DOUBLE CROCHET

Abbreviation: dc. ✛ . 1 turning ch required.

To make a double crochet insert the hook into the work from front to back picking up two strands of the stitch, yoh, draw loop through to front of the work [2 loops on hook], yoh, draw yarn through the 2 loops to bring work back to 1 loop - one double crochet (dc) made. See the 3 stages illustrated below.

making a double crochet

a

b

c

Crochet stitches vary in height. Double crochet is a short stitch. The crochet hook sits on top of the row being worked. It is necessary therefore to lift the hook to the start of the row to the right height. This is done by working turning chains. The number of turning chains required depends on the height of the stitches in the row to be worked next. Double crochet starts with one chain. This chain counts as a stitch and is the first stitch of the row.

To make a piece of double crochet fabric with straight sides, commence with a foundation chain. The number of stitches in the foundation ch should equal the number of dc stitches for the crochet fabric plus one. Make the first dc st of the row into the **third** ch from the hook remembering not to count the loop on the hook.

There is a smooth and a rough side to a chain. Have the smooth, 'embroidered chain' look towards you. Pick up the top 2 threads of the ch as you insert the hook into the

stitch. Make 1dc into each ch until all the ch have been used. The first row of dc is then complete.

Before turning the work, make the 1ch. Turn the work away from you into the palm of the hand. It is important that the 1ch is made before turning the work even though the 1ch is the first stitch of the next row, if the smooth side of the turning chain is to be available for the last stitch of the next row.

direction to turn work

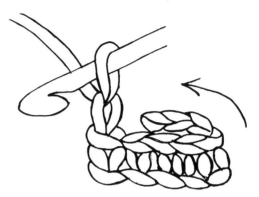

Insert the hook into the next stitch. Remember the first stitch is the turning chain and therefore the first dc is technically worked in the second stitch as shown below.

starting the next row

Cont working 1dc in each st to the end of the row. The very last st of a dc row is worked into the turning ch as shown below.

ending a
double crochet

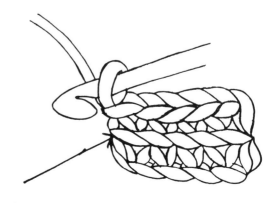

If working dc for the first time many find difficulty in keeping the correct number of stitches. This is usually because the turning chain at the end of the row has not been used. A good phrase to think about is "work to the last hole and then put 1dc into the 'knot'". The 'knot' being the chain.

It is possible to have the right number of stitches without the ends of the rows being straight but slightly scalloped. In this instance the hole directly below the turning chain at the beginning of the row has been used and the turning chain at the end of the row ignored.

When counting dc sts count the chain loops lying on the top of the stitches for the first row, but on subsequent rows count the holes at the bottom of the stitches.

It is easier to count rows two at a time. 2dc rows form what appear to be parallel lines with dashes between.

counting double crochet

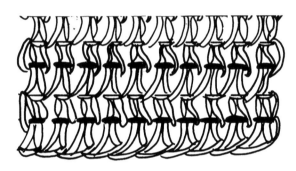

INCREASING (inc)

Increasing in crochet is easy. Simply put two stitches where you would normally put one.

    a   At the beginning of the row make 1dc into the first st which is sitting underneath the turning chain. That is the stitch from which the turning chain comes. As the turning chain is a stitch, by putting another one in the same place there are two stitches instead of the original one.

    b   At the end of the row put 2dc into the turning chain instead of the usual one so that you have an increase of one stitch.

    c   To increase a large number of stitches at the same time make a length of chain and work into it. NOTE: If a large number of stitches has to be added to both the beginning and the end of the row, it will be necessary to make a chain at the end of the row **plus** a turning chain, and **also** a length of chain at the **beginning** of the row of exactly the correct number. If this is not done, the increases will take place on different rows and in stitches of great height this can mean a difference of anywhere up to 15cm!

DECREASING (dec)

Decreasing is fractionally more difficult than increasing as two stitches are being worked together. Please **do not** use the 'miss one stitch' method unless you are looking for holes, steps, or other effects as a **design feature.**

    a   To dec at the beg of a row work in the 2sts after the turning ch. Insert hook into 2nd st of row, yoh, draw lp through (2 lps on hook), insert hook into third st of row, yoh, draw lp through (3 lps on hook), yoh, draw through all 3 lps. There is now 1ch top over 2dc sts, therefore 1 dec has been made.

    b   To dec at the end of the row, insert hook into the last hole (ie the next to the last stitch) and draw yarn through to the front (2 lps on hook). Now insert hook into the last hole, yoh, draw through to front, yoh, draw through all 3 lps - 1dec made.

    Some fabrics look better if 2sts are dec **before** the last st. That is the 2sts before the one worked in the turning chain. This will then give a similar look to the beg of the row when the turning chain is not used as a decrease.

    c   To dec by a large number of sts **at the beg of a row,** ss across the number of sts to be missed, 1ch (to lift hook), and cont with the crochet pattern. At the end of a row, simply stop, leaving the sts unworked, make 1ch, turn, and cont in the usual way.

DOUBLE CROCHET RIB

A ridged effect with an elasticated texture can be obtained by inserting the hook under the back loop of each double crochet stitch on every row after the foundation row. The foundation row in this case is a row of double crochet stitches into the foundation or base chain. All subsequent rows are worked into the back loop of the stitches only. A small number of stitches are required to make a welt or cuff.

The crochet rib is one fabric where the edges cause problems. The following method does overcome any irregularity at the sides of the work. This is very important if the rib is used as a welt or cuff for the side edge is the finished edge of the garment.

It is also worth noting that, as with knitting, the rib is worked on a smaller hook than the main body of the fabric.

In this pattern only, turn the work towards you at the end of the row after working the 1ch to lift. Insert hook into back loop of 3rd st down counting the turning ch as the first st. 1dc in back loop of each st to end. The very last st is worked into the back of the 'knot', that is the turning ch.

CRAB STITCH

There are many names for this stitch such as reverse double crochet, corded edge, rope stitch, Russian stitch, shrimp stitch, etc which is really a double crochet worked backwards. Crab stitches are worked from left to right instead of right to left, assuming you are right handed. Work them on the right side of a fabric as an edging or finishing row using a hook one size less than the one for the main fabric. The whipped look of this stitch is more pronounced if the right side is facing.

To make a crab stitch insert the hook in next stitch on the right, picking up 2 strands of yarn as normal. It is not necessary to work a lifting chain if the crab stitches are going in the round but work 1ch to lift on a straight piece. Collect the yarn from the ball by dropping the hook head onto the thread as shown in diagram. Bring the thread through to the front of the work tilting the hook upwards to make sure there are two loops on the hook otherwise it will be a backward ss. It is very easy at this stage to pull the yarn through to the front and also through the loop on the hook. Twist hook to a normal working position, yoh, draw through the 2 loops - one Crab stitch made.

crab stitch

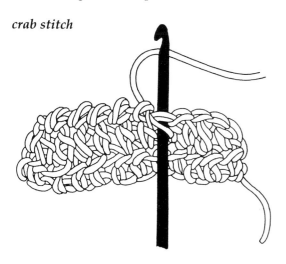

DOUBLE CROCHET BORDERS

Double crochet borders give a neat edge to crochet and knitting. A border at the top or bottom of a fabric using the same yarn and same size hook, use 1dc for each stitch. When adding a dc border to the side of the work it is necessary to have a ratio of 3sts to 4 rows if the work is going to lie flat. 1st per row will frill, 1st per 2 rows will create puckering.

It is not necessary to reduce the size of hook for the border. If the hook is reduced the corners will curl quite badly. There is a natural tendency for the top and bottom of the border to want to turn in or out, and a smaller hook will increase this tendency. If the borders curl try increasing the size of the hook, or using 2ch to turn. An alternative is to make sure that the turning chains are worked reasonably loosely so that they are still neat but have more length to them.

Crochet should not be pressed but occasionally the very edges of the borders do have to be. **Do not press** until you have pressed the tension square first. So many yarns look quite different after heat or/and water have been applied!

As a last resort rectify curling dc borders by running a piece of yarn from the corner to the main fabric as a stay stitch. Note broomstick crochet is a form of dc.

EXPERIMENTAL TECHNIQUES USING DOUBLE CROCHET

First 'play' with the ordinary dc to form straight sides, and also increasing and decreasing using smooth yarns and larger hooks first, then change the size of hook or type of yarn. Add a Crab stitch to the shaped piece leaving one edge unworked. Using approx 9ch (8sts) add a piece of dc rib to fit (slightly stretched) and attach with dc on the wrong side of work.

Also try working a piece of dc using a fine textured yarn and a large hook. Next try using the same yarn with different hooks for a rib.

Finally use a smooth yarn in a complementary colour and analyse the different effects. It is guaranteed you will not like them all!

CHAPTER FOUR
TREBLES

Abbreviation: tr. ⊤. 3 turning chain needed.

Only 50% of crochet workers require 3 turning ch for trebles unless working in fine crochet. Decide whether your crochet requires 2 or 3 turning ch but note, all patterns will recommend 3ch to turn so adjust for your own tension.

To make a treble, yoh, insert hook into work picking up two strands (ie the chain look on top of st), or of the foundation ch as given for dc. Yoh, draw thread through to front of work (3 lps on hook), yoh, draw through 2 lps, (2 lps on hook), yoh, draw thread through rem 2 lps (1 lp on hook) - 1tr made. Remember all stitches start and end with 1 lp on hook.

treble

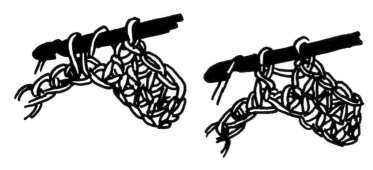

The height of a treble is twice that of a double crochet. The number of turning chain is always written as 3 but check whether the beginning of the row gapes and if so reduce it to 2. Work at **least** 8 rows before deciding.

Points to note when making a treble fabric

Commence with a foundation chain containing **only** 2 extra chains. Work first tr in fourth ch from hook to give the correct number of sts. Cont working 1tr in each ch to end. Work 3ch before turning. Turn into palm of hand as shown on pg 11 so the embroidered look of the chain will be facing when working into the turning ch of the next row. The easiest way to count trebles is to count the stems. Include the turning chain as one 'stem'.

Crochet stitches do not sit exactly on top of each other as they do in knitting for example. The hook is inserted a little to the left of the stem of the st for right handed crochet workers but because the work is turned for the next row this does not give a bias to a treble fabric. [Left-handed crochet is to the right of the st] If you have a bias at this stage it is probably because the hook is being placed in the space bet the sts and not in the st itself. It is important that all work is turned on each row or round unless you are working a pattern that uses st bias for a design effect.

If sts are too tall check that you have ALL the loops on the hook round the hook correctly. Knitters tend to lift the hook to the level of a knitting needle and that creates a taller stitch than required. Do ensure the hook is at a diagonal to the row and not level with the row.

Another reason for a loose tension is when the last loop on the hook has stretched before the hook is inserted into the work. This loop should be hugging the circumference of the hook in the same way as all other loops.

If the tension is too tight, check the hook is being held far enough away from the hook head so that the stitches are not being worked on the narrow part of the hook. Alternatively if you are nervous or under strain of any kind it is possible the yarn from the feed hand is stretching the yarn before it has worked the stitch. In that case do make sure the yarn is relaxed before it is worked otherwise the stitches being made will be smaller and with a thinner yarn than expected.

INCREASING IN TREBLES

    a   **At the beginning of the row** simply add 1tr in the st from which the turning ch comes, or, put 2tr in the st after the turning ch.

    b   **At the end of the row** put 2tr in the top of the turning ch, or put 2tr in the st before the last st which is a tr.

    c   **To increase by a large number of sts** at the beginning of a new row add the number of chains needed plus 2 for turning before the last row is complete. The first tr is worked in the 4th ch from the hook as on any first row of trebles worked from a chain.

        To increase by a large number of sts at the end of the new row, the number of chains needed have to be worked separately. Attach a small length of yarn to the first stitch of the row just worked ie the top of the turning ch. Make 1ch for each stitch to be added and fasten off. Watch a stitch is not lost in the fastening off. The chains can be worked over in the normal way as they are reached.

increasing trebles

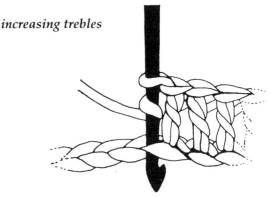

DECREASING IN TREBLES

    a   **At the beginning of a row:**
The turning ch should have been made and the work turned, yoh, insert hook into next st, yoh, draw

oop to front, yoh, draw through 2 lps on hook leaving 2 ps still on hook, yoh, insert hook into next st, yoh, draw through to front giving 4 lps, yoh, draw through 2 lps, (3 ps on hook), yoh, draw through 3 rem lps, giving 1 lp on hook ready for the next st.

decreasing in trebles

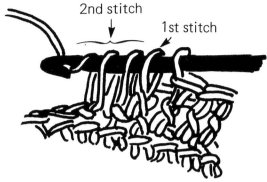

b   **At the end of a row:**
Work as above in the last 2sts. To make the edge look more like the decrease at the beginning of the row work in the 2sts prior to the last st placing 1tr in turning ch to look like the 3ch at the beginning of the row.

c   **A large number of sts:**
At the beginning of the row ss across the required number, work 3ch to lift hook to correct height, work tr as usual.
At the end of the row simply stop, leaving the required number unworked, 3ch, turn, and proceed in the normal manner.

SOME TREBLE FABRICS

SLIGHTLY OPEN

Wide but short (2ch to turn)

This is a treble fabric worked in exactly the same way as all other trebles but the insertion of the hook is quite different. Instead of picking up the top of the stitch (ie 2 strands) place hook between stems of trebles (ie in spaces between stitches which equals 3 strands). Because the stitches are shorter only 2ch is required for turning. Once turned the first stitch is put in the space between the turning chain and the next stitch to keep correct number of stitches.

trebles between trebles

'V' stitch (2ch to turn). Foundation chain to be divisible by 2 plus 1.

Here again the stitches are worked into the spaces between the stitches which means the hook is not lifted as far therefore work only 2ch to turn.
Row 1: 2tr in 5th ch from hook *miss 1ch, 2tr in next ch, rep from * to last 2sts, miss 1ch, 1tr in last st, 2ch, turn.
Row 2: *2tr in sp bet 2tr, rep from * to end, 1tr in turning ch, 2ch, turn.
Repeat row 2 for length required.

If increasing or decreasing check the 2tr groups sit inside each other to form vertical rows of interlocking 'V' stitches.

'V' stitch

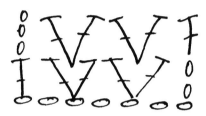

Crossed Trebles (2 ch to turn). Foundation chain to be divisible by 2.

Although the stitches are not being worked lower into the fabric, the crossing of the stitches one over the other shortens their length - hence only 2ch to turn.
Row 1: 1tr in 4th ch from hook, *miss 1ch, 1tr in next ch, 1tr in ch just missed, rep from * to last 2st, 2tr, 2ch, turn.
Row 2: 1tr, *miss 1tr, 1tr in next st, 1tr in st just missed, rep from * to last 2sts, 2tr, 2ch, turn.
Repeat row 2 for length required.

This pattern can be improved two ways, particularly if the sample is being submitted for scrutiny for a quality mark:

1. Because there is a border of 2tr up each side, the base and top of the sample will look unbalanced. A single row of dc or htr will help the overall balance of a square or rectangle.

2. A row of dc placed between the crossed trebles will keep the diagonal of the crosses in same direction.

crossed trebles

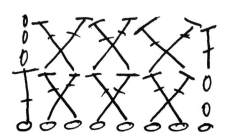

OPEN - Fabrics based on trebles

Spade pattern (3 turning ch). Foundation chain to be divisible by 6 plus 4.

Row 1: 1tr in 4th ch from hook, 1tr in each ch to end, 3ch, turn.
Row 2: *miss 2sts, 2tr 1ch 2tr in next st, miss 2sts, 1tr, rep from * to end, 3ch, turn.
Row 3: tr to end, 3ch, turn.
Row 4: 1tr in same place as turning ch, *miss 2sts, 1tr, miss 2sts, 1tr 1ch 1tr in next st, rep from * to last 6sts, miss 2sts, 1tr, miss 2sts, 2tr in last st, 3ch, turn.
Row 5: as row 3.
Repeat rows 2-5 incl for length required. To keep an even look to the pattern it is advisable to finish on either Row 3 or 5.

spade pattern

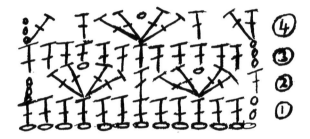

Divided Shell Pattern (3 turning ch). Foundation chain to be divisible by 8 plus 5.

Row 1: 1tr in 4th ch from hook, * miss 2ch, 5tr in next ch, miss 2ch, 1tr in next ch, 1ch, miss 1ch, 1tr in next ch, rep from * to last 7 sts, miss 2ch, 5tr in next ch, miss 2 ch, 2tr, 3ch, turn.
Row 2: 1tr, * 5tr in centre st of shell, 3tr in 1ch sp, rep from * to last shell, 5tr in group, 1tr in last 2sts, 3ch, turn.
Row 3: 1tr, * 5tr in centre of shell, 1tr in first st of group, 1ch, miss 1st, 1tr in last st of group, rep from * to last shell, 5tr in shell, 1tr in last 2st, 3ch, turn.
Rep rows 2 and 3 incl for length required. To put patt in its own frame Row 1 would need to be of htr or possibly dc. The last row should place htr over group, 1htr 1dc 1ss 1dc 1htr over shell.

divided shell pattern

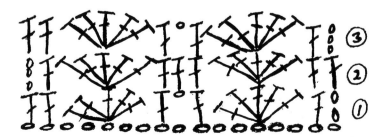

Filet Crochet

Filet crochet also comes under this heading. However, it is dealt with in more detail on page 33.

CHAPTER FIVE
TEXTURED STITCHES

There is a great deal of discussion about texture. To quote Jan Messent "Texture should be able to be felt by a blind person but a pattern can exist within a fabric without being felt". This is the correct text-book definition for general design but it is important to know that modern idiomatic interpretations of words do not necessarily use the purist or technical accuracy of terms used within any specialist area which are used in journalistic articles.

It is worthwhile to realise that the word **texture** in common usage is likely to mean 'heavily textured', therefore 'textured yarns' are usually fashion yarns incorporating slubs, knops, mohair strands, bouclé loops, etc., whilst textured fabrics normally mean the fabric has heavy texture created by the stitches.

Whilst the purist view is important and should be used wherever fibre art is involved, for the purpose of Part I Diploma in Crochet, (which is a practical, continuous assessment certificate) it is not the purist view but the specialist area definition that is required and used in this publication. Therefore please note that during Part I of the Diploma in Crochet only, when you are being requested to produce a textured fabric it is assumed that the fabric will incorporate medium to heavy texture created by the stitches and not be a fabric using yarns containing medium to heavy texture.

TEXTURED TREBLE FABRICS

Trebles are very suitable for introducing texture into a crochet fabric. By inserting the hook around the stem of a treble the stitch made will be either lifted forwards or pushed backwards. Bobbles create texture also, giving a lumpy embossed look and feel to a fabric. Ball-shaped textures are made by putting groups of stitches in the same place. Texture can be introduced into a crochet fabric in a similar way with the Tunisian crochet [see page 27] or by using long stitches between short stitches [see page 20].

Use of raised trebles or raised long trebles can produce fabrics similar to the knitted fisherman's gansey or aran sweater during the time of making the fabric and not as surface crochet afterwards. Similar effects can be achieved with embellishing, which is an area covered in a later book.

On the whole crochet should not use more yarn than any knitting pattern and this applies to aran-style crochet also. Knitted aran sweaters are much heavier than stocking stitch sweaters and equally crochet aran-style sweaters are heavier than other fabrics as it is the nature of the design. It should be remembered when ordering or buying yarn to make the raised treble stitch designs that more yarn will be needed.

Making a Raised Treble Front abbreviation RtrF 2 chain to turn is required as the hook is placed into the work around the stem of the stitch and not in the top.

This stitch will pull the fabric towards you and therefore is referred to as a raised treble **front**. It does not mean it will be on the right side of the fabric automatically, only pushed forwards.

Yoh, insert hook from right to left round stem of st below, yoh, draw hook from behind stem (3 lps now on hook), *yoh, draw through 2 lps, rep from * once. A raised treble front has been made.

raised treble front

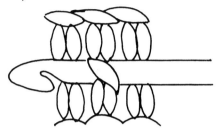

Making a Raised Treble Back abbreviation RtrB 2chain to turn.

This stitch will pull the fabric away from you and therefore is referred to as a raised treble back. Work this in a similar way to a RtrF but insert hook from right to left round the stem of the treble from behind the fabric. The working of the stitch will push the stem of the treble to the back.

raised treble back

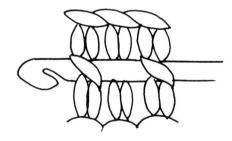

RAISED TREBLE RIB

An elasticated welt or band can be made using raised trebles. It is important to realise the chain from which the first row of trebles is made, is not elastic therefore all ribs must be worked away from the main fabric and not begin with the chain edge of the Rtr rib.

Work a length of chain to equal sts needed plus 2.
Row 1: 1tr in 4th ch from hook, 1tr in each st to end, 2ch, turn.
Row 2: *1RtrF,1RtrB, rep from * to last st, place a Rtr round last st by inserting hook into the space in whatever direction comes next, 2ch, turn.
Row 3: Look whether the next st is pushed back or

forwards. If back commence with a RtrB, if forwards commence with a RtrF. Keep all Rtr in a continuous line. Repeat until a sufficient length has been made.

raised treble rib

Variations

1. Work a rib using 2RtrF, 1RtrB
2. Work a rib using 2RtrF, 2RtrB
3. 'moss stitch' effect is by working 1RtrF, 1RtrB as in a single Rtr rib, but work the RtrB on the stitches pushing forward and the RtrF on the stitches pushing backward.
4. A basket weave effect can be obtained by working 2RtrF,2RtrB in the way described in 3.

moss stitch　　　　*basket weave*

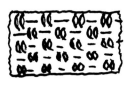 

BOBBLES

One of the difficulties with crochet is the lack of standardisation of stitch names. The term cluster is given to many stitches where stitches are drawn together at the top. Throughout this book all stitches gathered together at the top will be a cluster whether the stitches sit as a group in one stitch at the bottom or are spread over a number of stitches.

3tr cluster Abbreviation 3trcl ! The number of turning chain is to be the same as the height of the stitch between the clusters. If a 3trcl is put into a dc row only 1ch is required, but if the 3trcl is put in a tr row, 3ch will be needed.

a {all sts worked in the same place} yoh, insert hook into st, yoh, pull through to front (3 lps on hook), yoh, pull through 2 lps, *yoh, insert hook into same st, yoh, pull through to front, yoh, pull through 2 lps, rep from * once, (4 lps on hook), yoh, pull through rem 4 lps.

b using 3 consecutive sts as in the case of a chevron fabric. Work as above but replace 'same st' for 'next st'. This is NOT a bobble but follows naturally from (a)

cluster in 1st　　　　*cluster over 3sts*

 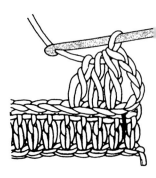

POPCORNS

Clusters can flatten with use, particularly in soft acrylics and wool yarns, but popcorns retain their texture even after pressing. Pressing crochet is NOT recommended except for firm mercerized cottons and in other isolated cases.

Make with RS of crochet facing - work 6tr into the same st remove hook from st and insert it from front to back of the first of the 6tr just made. Collect the loose loop and pull lp through to the front. Cont crocheting along the row in the normal way.

popcorns

There are two variations to the working of popcorns:
a) add 1ch after popcorn is made to ensure stitches are not lost on return row. It is debatable whether this is a correct method as there may be too many stitches in the next row and also there can be a change of appearance to the fabric with the added chain depending upon the yarn and the sts following.

b) work the popcorn in a row of shorter stitches such as dc or htr to give an even greater bump than when incorporated in a row of trebles.

PUFF STITCH

The only claim to being part of the treble family is that the yarn is wrapped over the hook once before the hook is inserted into the fabric. Working on the definition that "tr is 'throw round'" a puff stitch is really a collection of trebles placed in the same stitch which are unworked until the end.

To make a puff stitch (yoh, insert hook into st, lift hook to a horizontal position so that the yarn coming through the stitch is lifted away from the stitch, creating a large loop)3times, yoh, pull through all 7 loops on hook. The puff stitch is much more effective if worked in rows of shorter stitches. If it's not possible to place puff stitches into rows of short stitches it may be necessary to work the brackets 4, 5 or even 6 times depending upon the thickness of the yarn.

puff stitch

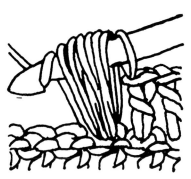

Where the yarn is wrapped over the hook more than once before the hook is inserted into the stitch, the stitch becomes longer. All the loops are removed in twos, in the same way as they are removed when working an ordinary treble. To repeat, all crochet begins and ends with one loop on the hook. This loop is not counted as a stitch but is only counted when working a stitch where the loops on the hook need to be checked. To make a longer stitch, the yarn is simply wrapped round more times.

DOUBLE TREBLE
Abbreviation dtr ‡ 4 chain to turn.

To make a dtr, * (yoh)twice, insert hook into work under 2 strands in normal way, yoh, draw yarn to front of work [4 loops on hook], (yoh, draw through 2 lps)3 times - 1dtr made.

double treble

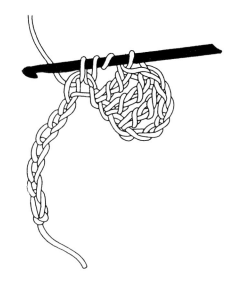

TRIPLE TREBLE
Abbreviation trtr ‡ 5 chain to turn

To make a trtr, * (yoh)3 times, insert hook into work under 2 strands in normal way, yoh, draw yarn to front of work [5 loops on hook], (yoh, draw through 2 lps)4 times - 1trtr made.

triple treble

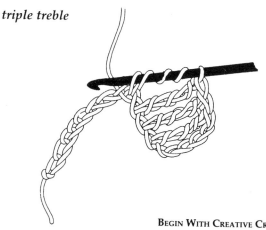

QUADRUPLE TREBLE
Abbreviation quadtr 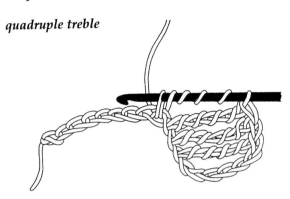6 chain to turn

To make a quadtr, * (yoh)4 times, insert hook into work under 2 strands in normal way, yoh, draw yarn to front of work [6loops on hook], (yoh, draw through 2 lps)5 times - 1 quadtr made.

quadruple treble

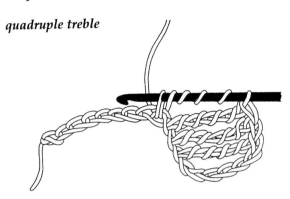

INCREASING IN LONG TREBLES

a)   **Increasing by 1st**
       Simply work another long treble in the same stitch as the previous long treble made.

b)   **Increasing by large numbers**
       Work as described on page 14 but remember to add 1 extra ch for a dtr, 2ch extra for a trtr, and 3ch extra for a quadtr ie the length of turning chain being made for the start of the next row.

DECREASING IN LONG TREBLES

a)   **Decreasing by 1st**
       Work first st until 2 lps are left on hook, work next st until 3 lps are left on hook, yoh, draw through all 3 lps.

b)   **Decreasing by a large number**
       Work as described on page 15.

EXPERIMENTING WITH LONG TREBLES

Using an aran thickness of yarn and a 5.00mm or 5.50mm crochet hook, practise the different long trebles and compare them with samples made previously in dc and tr. If the samples have been worked in the same piece with straight sides, one section of sts on top of another, the fabric will become wider as the stitches become longer. This characteristic has to be taken into consideration if long trebles are being used as a fabric which does not include shorter stitches. From height of trtr, it will be necessary to use either a larger hook for the foundation chain (not the turning chain) or work the foundation chains looser. Obviously everyone's tension is not exactly the same and therefore the stitch where hook sizes need to be considered will vary from dtr to quadtr.

The aim is to have all the stitches standing vertically in rows and not leaning away from each other. There are two points of working where the tension needs to be controlled more rigidly in a fabric using longer trebles:

        a) with lp on hook, before yoh, check that lp has not stretched, place a finger on this lp to stop it becoming looser.
        b) whilst wrapping the yarn round hook where multiple wrapping can create looseness, keep a finger on each yoh as it occurs until lps are worked off this gives greater control and the stitches will then stay even and erect.

LONG TREBLE FABRICS

There are certain disadvantages to using only long trebles as a fabric particularly when wrapping the yarn three or more times round the hook.   These are:

        1. There is little substance to such a fabric and unless it is worked in a cotton or other non-elastic yarn on a smaller hook, it has a tendency to lose its shape.

        2. The stitches easily catch on objects such as door handles etc

        3. Sleeves of long trebles droop and can get in the way during wear.

However the advantages are:
        1. It grows very quickly and is most suitable for stoles, scarves, bed- jackets, etc worked in a fluffy yarn.

        2. If one row of long trebles is worked occasionally in a fabric of another firmer pattern, it adds interest to the overall effect as a contrasting texture.

        3. It is ideal for using as a base stitch to allow ribbon, elastic, cords, etc to be threaded through, either for decorative or utility effect.

TEXTURED STITCHES

One way to use long trebles is to put them in a row of shorter stitches to give a textured effect.

As mentioned previously there is no right or wrong side to crochet until it is made to have a right or a wrong side. With the bouclé stitch, the work has a smooth side and a rough side. The rough side is the right side in this fabric. When crocheting the bouclé stitch and all other stitches where texture is created by including long stitches between short stitches, the wrong or smooth side of the work should be facing to allow the tall stitches to bend away from the smooth side and create a variety of lumps and bumps. Usually the roughness is pronounced if you bend the taller stitches behind and closer to the base of the row being worked with a finger of the yarn hand before the short stitch is made.

TEXTURED TREBLE FABRICS

Bouclé Stitch

Make a length of chain which gives an odd number of sts.
Work 1 row of a basic stitch such as tr, htr, or dc.
Patt row: [Note this has the wrong side of fabric now facing], 1ch, turn, *1dtr,1dc, rep from * to end.
VARIATION: can be 1trtr, 1dc.
> or 1tr, 1ss.

Raised Fan Edge [multiple of 5 plus 2]

Wherever the raised fans are placed, the previous row to the patt row should be a row of trebles. Anything smaller makes the fans gather up too much, anything larger creates a loose tension which tends to distort the shape.

Patt row: 1ch, turn, * miss 4sts, 1RquadtrF 1RtrtrF 1RdtrF 1RtrF all into next st with the quadtr at base of st, 1dc into top of **same** st, rep from * to last st, 1dc in last st.

Aran-style

It is much easier to get an Aran-style effect in crochet by using the raised long trebles to lean over stitches to produce cable effects. Patterns for these are in another 'Creative World of Crochet' book but there is no reason why you cannot experiment with this idea to create your own patterns.

COLOUR AND TEXTURE IN LONG TREBLES

The beauty of using long trebles to create changes in stripes of colour is endless. A little bit of imagination and experimentation can produce some wonderful coloured, textured fabrics that will lead into all forms of fashion garments, household items, wearable art, hangings, etc.

As shown previously with raised stitches, long trebles do not need to be worked into the tops of other stitches or in the spaces made by chains, they can also be worked around the stem to lift stitches forwards and backwards. However, if the stitches are worked in rows lower down than the one usually used, this idea can be utilised for colour blending effects. The Box pattern below uses long raised trebles to break a simple straight stripe into geometric shapes. For a strong visual effect use two contrasting colours in the same type of yarn.

Boxes - chain to be divided by 4

Row 1: In M, 1tr in 4th ch from hook, tr to end, 3ch, turn
Row 2: In M, tr to end, change to C, 3ch, turn,
Row 3: In C, tr to end, 3ch, turn
Row 4: In C, tr to end, change to M, 3ch, turn
Row 5: 1tr, *1RquadtrF 3rows below [ie in last row of M], 3tr, rep from * to last 2st, 2tr.
Rep rows 2-5 incl to required length.

Please note the quadruple treble is a stitch, therefore there will be one unworked chain top lying behind the quadtr. If this is worked into there will be increases.

Two-colour Ripple Stitch - chain to be divided by 2+1

Row 1: In M, 1tr in 4th ch from hook, tr to end, 1ch, turn
Row 2: In M, 1dc in each st to end, change to C, 3ch, turn.
Row 3: In C, *1RdtrF in tr row, 1tr, rep from * to end, 1ch, turn.
Row 4: In C, 1dc in each st to end, change to M, 3ch, turn.
Row 5: In M, 1tr, *1RdtrF in tr row, 1tr, rep from * to last st, 1tr in last st, 1ch, turn.
Rep row 2-5 incl to required length.

EXPERIMENTING WITH COLOUR AND TEXTURE

There are many two row patterns where there is a textured stitch pattern on one row and the alternate rows are of a basic stitch. As crochet does not need to be turned on every row but can quite easily be turned every two rows the textured row can be in contrast and the plain row in main. Note that this could alter the look of the stitches slightly and either replace one of the textured rows with a simple dc row, or alternatively work the textured stitches so that they are coming towards you as you work and not away from you. The second option takes a little more time and often requires a shorter stitch between the ones creating the chunky effect.

A general guide working with fashion and highly textured yarns is to work with a very simple stitch and keep to a relatively flat fabric as any addition of heavily textured stitches are lost in the yarn. Just occasionally a design can require the reverse to occur and below is an adaptable design which can make a short waistcoat, long edge-to-edge sleeveless jacket or a tabard.

TEXTURED WAISTCOAT

The pattern is <u>not complete.</u> That is it has not been written in the way a pattern is written in a pattern leaflet obtained from a yarn shop. The principles behind the design are simple and are outlined here so that you can use these principles to make your own designs, or adapt this one in anyway you desire.

a   it is a basic rectangular shape, which allows the imagination freedom without having to cope with increases and decreases.

b   Where a textured stitch is introduced it is worked in a textured yarn which doubles the 'chunky', 'bobbly', 'hairy' properties of the yarn being incorporated.

c   The main pieces [which are in stripes], have the stripes worked from side to centre back, giving an optically narrowing and lengthening effect to the figure.

d   The final borders are the means used to ensure a good fit.

shaping of waistcoat

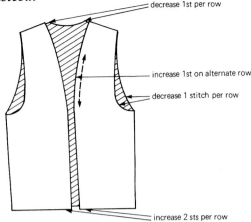

decrease 1st per row

increase 1st on alternate row

decrease 1 stitch per row

increase 2 sts per row

As this is not a crochet pattern in the accepted sense the following points may be of use:

1   The length can be adjusted by adding pairs of stitches, or removing pairs of stitches

2   The fabric is not made using any one spinner's range of yarn, but by mixing many makes - British, American and other imported yarns. Discontinued lines or the oddments box ease the cost.

3   Remember all textured stitches are worked on the wrong side except when working raised treble stitches. To avoid bias it is therefore advisable to work the rows between the textured rows, on the Right Side.

4.   The whole is worked in DDK but two DK yarns can be worked together or alternatively three strands of 4-ply can be used to give the DDK thickness. This adds to the possible colour combinations, shading etc within the garment.
Note: If a thinner version is required work in DK through-out but double the stitches and use a 4.00mm hook. Preferably use a few stitches less and work in DK and a 4.50mm hook.

5.   Each row of the main pieces can be worked in different yarns and it is not necessary to make the two pieces symmetrical. However, if this is your first adventure in colour crochet and texture it is suggested that you make both pieces alike, working one row on one piece and then the same row on the other piece so there is no likelihood of insufficient yarn!

6.   Choose the colour for the borders and waistband carefully, as this is the major contribution to the overall aesthetic appearance of the waistcoat, holding the oddments of colour and texture together as a complete whole.

7.   If the garment is being made for a fuller figure aim to have the lightest shades in the centre back and centre front, grading to the darkest shades under the arms, this combined with the downward stripes will be very figure flattering.

8.   Again for the fuller figure do not make a waistband unless the wearer has a smaller bust than hip, a narrow waist and with most of the fullness on the hips. Usually a long line style is the most flattering.

9.   The garment launders well in a cold water wash, and there are special detergents on the market to make this possible.

SHORT WAISTCOAT

Use a 7.00mm hook for size 87-92cm. ## indicates the place where extra rows can be inserted into the pattern for larger sizes.
Thickness of yarn should be DDK (slightly thicker than an Aran)

TO MAKE

Left Side Body Piece (Centre back panel)
Read notes above before commencing.
Make 77ch in a smooth yarn
Row 1: 1tr in 4th ch from hook, tr to end, [75st]. Break off yarn.
Row 2: [becomes wrong side], join in a mohair yarn, *4trcl, 1ss, rep from * to end. Break off yarn.
Row 3: With a smooth yarn and wrong side still facing work 1 row htr, 2ch, turn.
Row 4: tr to end. Break off yarn
Row 5: With RS facing join in a bouclé yarn. *1RtrF, 1dc, rep from * to end. Break off yarn.
Row 6: With WS facing and a strong contrasting colour in a smooth yarn work 1 row tr. Break off yarn.
Row 7: With RS facing and a medium textured yarn, *1 elongated tr (one tr looped up so that it does not distort the fabric) worked into the top of the Rtr on row 5, 1dc, rep from * to end. Break off yarn.
Row 8: With RS facing and a smooth yarn work 1 row tr. Fasten off yarn.
Row 9: With WS facing join in mohair yarn * 1tr, 1ss, rep from * to end. Break off yarn
Row 10: With RS facing and smooth yarn work 1 row tr. Break off yarn. ##
Row 11: With RS facing join in a smooth multicoloured yarn (two or three thin yarns plyed will be suitable) *1RtrF, 1tr, rep from * 15 times. Break off yarn.
Work on these 33sts.
Row 12: With WS facing join in a bouclé yarn *1tr, 1ss, rep from * to end. Break off yarn
Row 13: With RS facing and a smooth yarn work 1 row tr. Break off yarn.
Row 14: With WS facing join in a chenille yarn, *1tr, 1ss, rep from * to end. Break off yarn.
Row 15: With RS facing and a smooth yarn work 1 row tr. Break off yarn.

Right side body piece (Centre Back Panel)

Work as left side body piece until Row 10 (and any extensions) have been completed. Work Rows 11-15 incl on last 33sts with RS facing. Join the two pieces together with crab stitch on RS, using a textured yarn. Alternatively stitch them together decoratively.

ide Borders

n a smooth DDK yarn and 7.00mm hook work 3 rows in
lc. Lose 1st on every row at the shoulder point by dc2tog.
Place wrong side of back and front together and on RS
join the 2 pieces with Crab stitch for 15sts. Do not break
off yarn but continue round the armhole with Crab Stitch
on the RS missing every 5th st for a good fit.   Fasten off.

Waistband

for a 72cm waist

#[at this point extra sts can be added to fit a larger waist]

Work 95htr evenly into the crochet of the main piece at
waist level using a smooth DDK yarn.
Next row: 2ch, 1RtrF, 1RtrB, rep from * to end.
Rep this row until 7-9cm has been worked. Do not break
off yarn but continue to work front border.

Front Border

Dc up front edge to shoulder point, dc across back neck
using no more than 10sts, dc down other front, 1ch, turn
(occasionally requires 2ch at this point). Work a further
4 rows dc losing 1st on each row at shoulder points and
putting 3 buttonholes in waistband, by missing every 6th
st. Note only the border attached to the rib of the
waistband fastens. Break off yarn. Stitch on buttons to
correspond with the buttonholes.

LONG-LINE EDGE-TO-EDGE JACKET

To make a long-line edge-to-edge, jacket make 135ch
instead of 77.   The jacket can be longer or shorter as
desired by adding or omitting 4sts [2 for the back and 2 for
the front length].
Omit the rib and replace with a band which can be a
continuation of the front border.
Work two additional pieces for the front of the jacket in
the same way as the centre back panel.   It will be
necessary to add 2 or 4 rows more than those for the back
of the waistcoat.

TABARD

To make a tabard, work exactly as the long line but work
2 extra rows for the left-hand side and also for the right-
hand side at the front in place of the front border.
Join as for Centre back join of waistcoat.
Work border round the neck.
Add a border to the base.

This could be made shorter (as for the waistcoat) and a rib
worked for the welt.

CHAPTER SEVEN
BROOMSTICK CROCHET

Other names for broomstick crochet are:-
     lattice loop
     witchcraft lace
     jiffy lace
these are rarely seen and seem to have been names chosen
by one person during the pattern writing of broomstick
crochet, or have come from one very small district.

Broomstick crochet is a way of incorporating large loops
of yarn into an openwork textile using a crochet hook and
thick knitting needle. Before the 20mm and 25mm knitting pins were easily obtained, a broom handle sandpa-
pered down to a glass-like finish, or an imported Whiz
pin was used. The advent of the larger sizes of knitting
needles makes it possible to vary the height of the loops.
For example 12mm and 15mm knitting needles are available and these work well being sized between the 10mm
needle that is used for fine cotton and the 20mm.

On the Continent a flat piece of wood or plastic was used
to regulate the size of loops but this has the problem of
cutting the thread when a fragile fibre is used.

Broomstick crochet is only a stitch pattern using a double
crochet stitch and a chain. It has one basic principle but
as with all things this pattern can be used imaginatively.

THE PRINCIPLE OF BROOMSTICK

1.   Make a chain of sufficient length, after first trying
a tension square. The chain should be divisible by the
number of loops to be in the groups. For example if the
groups of loops are to be four, then the chain should be
divisible by four, eg 20,24,28,32, etc, if the groups are in
fives then the chain should be divisible by five, eg
20,25,30,35, etc.

2.   Pick up the loops onto a knitting needle, whiz pin,
or any other aid to keep the loops even. At this stage they
are easy to count.

3.   Remove the loops in groups using 1dc for each
loop removed (see pg 25)

CHOICE OF MATERIALS

Choose the hook for the yarn. For instance when working
an aran type yarn use a hook around 5.50mm and when
using a 4-ply yarn use a 3.50 or 4.0mm hook. The width
of the broomstick bears no relation to the hook size.

As broomstick crochet has an easily recognised stitch
pattern it is often chosen to show the pattern within the
item as its design feature. Because of this a clean crisp
yarn rather than a slub or fluffy yarn is a good choice in
making the stitch a prominent feature. However if it is
a lacy but warm item that is being made, lightweight

textured fashion yarns are most suitable.

The thickness of the 'broomstick' or knitting needle will depend on two things. First there is a difficulty in using a small knitting needle with a thick yarn, but it is simple to use a large knitting needle and a thin yarn. Secondly, the thicker the knitting needle or regulator, the longer the loops therefore the loops on the bigger needle have a tendency to catch more easily particularly with the finer yarns. This is an important point to remember when designing for babies and young children.

Because of the openness of the fabric, it is best to avoid zips, hooks and eyes, Velcro and press studs, as fasteners. Suitable fasteners for a broomstick garment are ties, with buttons if a firmer band has been added. An elastic insertion and a separate belt are also useful for broomstick pattern garments.

TENSION

Measuring the tension of broomstick is not too difficult but it is important to know how the article being made in broomstick is to be used. For instance a loose bedcover will come out exactly the size of the tension worked. However, if the broomstick crochet is to be for a summer blouse you may find you prefer to make the blouse a little smaller [approx 5cm] so that the body can show the beauty of the design of the pattern. Alternatively if the yarn being used is quite fine without much stretch, you may prefer to make the top very loose so that it can drape.

JOINING YARN IN BROOMSTICK

Because of the distance the yarn has to travel over the knitting needle before it is anchored into a double crochet stitch, the following method of joining yarn can be used without waste and without detection within the fabric.

joining in yarn

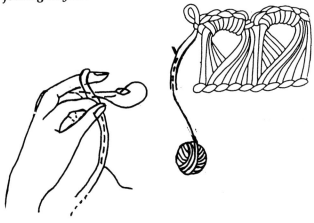

Thread the end of the yarn from the new ball into a sewing needle or tapestry needle. Stretch the end of the old yarn over the fingers and oversew the new yarn through the old yarn in the opposite direction as shown. Remove needle from new yarn and pull two ends gently until they

become tight and are approximately the same thickness as the original thread. The length of the oversewing should be **at least** 7cm long and the crochet can continue as though it is a continuous thread. Should there be any ugly ends of yarn sticking out of the join as shown, snip them closely with a pair of sharp scissors.

JOINING SEAMS IN BROOMSTICK

There are two excellent ways of joining the broomstick rows together.

1. **With a sewing needle**

Thread yarn into needle and attach to start of seam. Oversew three or four times in the double crochet part or foundation chain only. Carry the yarn behind the pattern to the next dc row in the patt, making certain the carrying thread is not too tight or the work will gather. The loose thread does not show as it fits into the strands of the broomstick crochet as part of the pattern.

2. **Using a crochet hook**

This is particularly good if there is ordinary crochet between the rows of broomstick. Work 2dc through both edges of crochet to join.

Pull the loop up until it is the height of the loops in the broomstick pattern, and continue with a further 2dc in the solid section of broomstick. The strands of the loose chain or loop will "disappear" in the open part of the pattern.

Joining bases of broomstick

It is advisable to crochet these together using the chains from which the first row was worked [ie the foundation chain] in a decorative way. This is used as a centre back in some patterns.

Joining tops of broomstick

The work looks much neater if only the centre stitches of each group of loops are sewn or crocheted together, rather than using all the stitches, particularly when taking loops off in groups of four or more.

Armhole edging

There are of course, many variations but 1dc 2tr 1dc worked in the looped part of the crochet makes a neat and interesting finish to the work. This avoids using the dc part of the pattern.

TO WORK BROOMSTICK CROCHET

Begin a sample piece of broomstick on a large needle, [eg

25mm], a ball of aran-type yarn to give a good stitch definition, and a 5.50mm crochet hook.

Work as follows:

1.   Make 20ch loosely

chain   *loop on knitting needle*

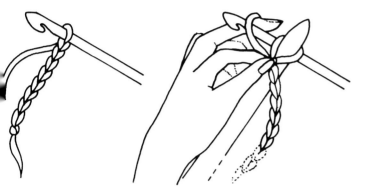

2.   Draw loop on hook large enough to fit snugly round knitting needle. Hold the knitting needle firmly, ideally anchored between the thighs as this avoids putting the body on a twist. However, it can be wedged between the arm of a chair and your thigh, or placed under one arm.

3.   Insert hook into next chain, yoh and draw through to front. Extend loop as before and place on the broomstick.

adding loops to broomstick

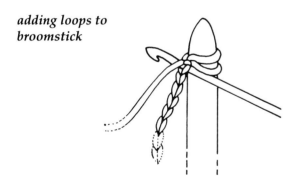

4.   Work each chain this way until all the chains have been used. In this instance there should be 20 loops on the needle.

loops on needle showing group to be removed

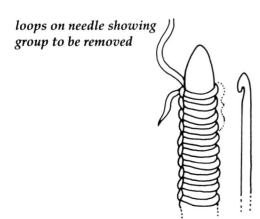

5.   The ridge of the chain will be at the LH side of the needle if you are a righthanded worker. Give the broomstick a half turn so that the working yarn lies behind the needle. Remove loops by inserting hook into first four loops and with the hook pointing in the same direction as the tip of the knitting needle. Yoh, draw yarn through loosely. It is important the yarn stays on top of the group of loops to avoid the side of the loops being pulled down towards the starting chain

removing first group of loops

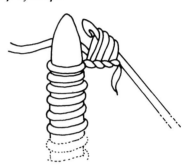

6   Yoh, pull yarn through loop already on hook, 1ch made. This does NOT count as a stitch as all crochet has to begin and end with a loop on the hook. This chain acts in the capacity of a slip knot when commencing any crochet work.

7   Make 4dc through centre of the group of loops. NOTE: It is 4dc here because four loops have been removed.

replacing loops with dc

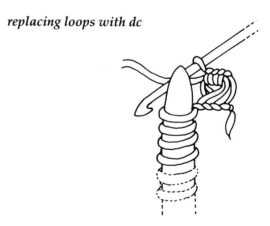

8.   Remove next 4 lps inserting hook as before. Work 4dc in these 4 lps. It is easier if you place the thumb of the hand holding the knitting needle into the group of loops, to ensure an even size loop throughout. As there is already 1 lp on the hook when you remove the second and subsequent groups, there is no need to make a chain to produce a loop as was necessary in the first group.

9.   Cont rep step 8 until all loops have been removed.

10.   Replace lps by giving the needle another half turn. Lift loop on hook and place over needle. *Place hook into next dc [the first dc has a loop on the broomstick already]. Make sure hook is inserted under two strands. Yoh, draw yarn through, extend and place on broomstick. Repeat from * to end.

Work steps 8 & 9 once more. Cont working steps 10, 8 and 9 until the work measures the required length.

the look of broomstick

INCREASING AND DECREASING

Increasing in broomstick is very easy - simply add more dc to the group.

Decreasing is equally easy - simply put less dc in the group.

It will take 2 full pattern rows to complete either an increase or a decrease. For instance in a pattern taking the loops off in 4, the group will have only 2dc in the 4 loops for a decrease, and on the next row there will be 6 loops left. Put 4 dc into these 6 loops and a full group of 4 loops has been removed with a pleasing slope, rather than a step. Adding a group of 4 loops is worked in reverse. Put 6dc in the group of 4 loops but on the next row when there are 6 loops, place 4dc in 4 loops and 4dc in 2 loops.

Odd numbers can be worked in a similar way placing 3dc in a group of 5 first and then on the next row using the full 5dc once more.

To add lots of small increases to create a frill, an extra dc can be placed in alternate groups. The next row then has groups made of 4 loops followed by 5 loops if the original pattern was being worked in 4. This will give a frilled look and is ideal for adding gentle fullness to a blouse from the waist to the hip level.

BROOMSTICK FOR THE HOME

Broomstick crochet is ideal for curtains, bedcovers, and edgings on towels etc.

ADDING ORDINARY CROCHET

To incorporate crochet into a broomstick pattern it is necessary to adjust the width of the straight crochet rows to avoid frilling. There are two ways of doing this:

1.   Change the hook size

As this incurs a drop of up to 4 sizes of hook, there is a noticeable change in the look of the stitch fabric, as the dc in the broomstick look quite slack or alternatively the crochet between the broomstick becomes stiff like cardboard.

2.   Change the number of stitches

Use the same hook throughout but if loops are being removed in groups of 5 as an example, use only the top 4 stitches of the group leaving the stitch lying between the groups unworked. When removing groups in fours omit 1st in every 2 groups and also work the broomstick with one hook size larger than the crochet between the broomstick. However, if taking the groups off in 3 lose 1st for 2 groups but do not change the size of the hook.

CHAPTER EIGHT
TUNISIAN CROCHET

Tunisian crochet is usually worked on a hook that is as long as a knitting needle. During the late 1980's there have been difficulties in obtain Tunisian hooks, however it is possible to get the traditional style hook in a range 2.50mm to 7.00mm. Flexi-hooks are available in the same range plus 8.00mm and 10.00mm sizes. The flexi-hook is an ordinary length crochet hook with a plastic wire attached, rather like the circular knitting needles. The end of the wire contains a moveable stopper so that the stitches do not slip and drag the weight of the work out of shape.

Tunisian crochet produces a fabric not unlike a woven textile. It appears to be a cross between knitting and weaving but the actions to make it are a cross between knitting and crochet. The loops are picked up in one direction as though picking up stitches in knitting and then crocheted off in the other direction.

Until recently, Tunisian crochet has been much ignored especially in the United Kingdom. One of the main reasons for this was because many patterns recommended the same size hook for Tunisian crochet as for knitting. The finished work is then stiff and often heavy having taken a great deal of yarn. In this state however it is suitable for rugs and upholstery fabrics. The use of larger hooks has made it ideal for fashion.

Tunisian crochet does not contradict the principle that all crochet starts with a loop and ends with a loop no matter how complicated the process in between. Tunisian crochet starts with a slip knot, followed by a chain (unless the stitches are picked up directly from another fabric). The Tunisian row comprises picking up the loops in one direction and removing those loops to bring the work back to just one loop on the hook, in another direction. A word of warning! When reading Tunisian crochet patterns, do check how the designer has written the instructions. Some designers describe the picking up and taking off of the loops as only one row of Simple Stitch, whilst others think of the process as two rows. Within the pages of this book, the picking up and taking off of the loops will be considered as one row to fit in with the principle of crochet commencing and ending with one loop on the hook.

Another confusing point about Tunisian crochet is the variety of names given to it. Originally in Great Britain it was called tricot, loosely translated as French knitting, or tricoter and even tricot écossais. This name gave rise in some places to assume that Tunisian crochet came from Scotland. In America the name given to this crochet textile is Afghan crochet. None of the names given, relates to the country of origin!

TUNISIAN SIMPLE STITCH

Use a hook 1 size smaller than the Tunisian hook, make a chain. The length of the chain should be the number of stitches required for a row of Tunisian simple stitch. In patterns it is the amount given in the tension check or in the working pattern. In a pattern there is no need to decide how many chain are needed, as these are written in the instructions.

To Work

Stage I

Insert hook into second chain, pick up only the top strand of the chain and not 2 lps as is the case in ordinary crochet.

stage 1

Stage II

It is easier to check the number of stitches at this point rather than trying to count them when the work is back to one loop. Yoh, pull through 1 lp [this is the equivalent of 1 turning chain, to raise the hook into position] *yoh, pull through 2 loops, rep from * to end of row. As seen in sketch the yarn collected in the hook head will pull through the working loop just made and the next loop at (a). This row makes a base from which to start the Tunisian simple stitch fabric. Some patterns refer to the whole of the above procedure as the foundation row or rows, but there is no obvious advantage to separating the first row from the rest.

stage 2

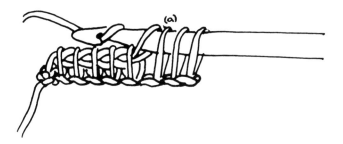

Stage III

Picking up the vertical strand in front of the stitches for the next row of loops is rather like making a row of knitting. Do not make a turning chain at the start of the picking up procedure. Think of the pick-up process as following knitting principles and the take-off process as following crochet principles.

The action of picking up loops on one row and taking them off on another gives a vertical strand to the front of the work. This vertical strand becomes available once the base or first row has been completed. The loop on the hook is the stitch for the first vertical strand, insert hook into next strand as shown in the figure below. Yoh, pull through [2 loops on hook]. Cont until all vertical strands have been used including the one at the end marked (b).

stage 3

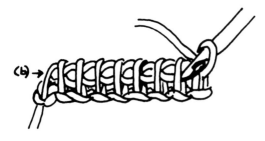

<u>Stage IV</u>

Complete the row by making 1ch. Think of the loops on the hook as an enormously long treble and work accordingly, collecting yarn in hook head and removing 2 lps at a time until only 1 lp remains on hook.

TUNISIAN PATTERNS

Even if only basic stitches are being used it is useful to look and see if you can change the pattern to get a better finish. For instance, work more than one pattern piece together to avoid seams.

Points to look for:

1.   The work leaning, particularly slanting to the right:

Action: Check you are going into the second vertical strand and not using the first strand

Action: Check you are picking up the vertical strand at the front of the fabric and not going through the work from front to back

2.   Insufficient stitches. That is losing stitches on each row:

Action: Check you are picking up the last strand (b) in figure. Alternatively check that it is the vertical strands and not
the horizontal strands that are being picked up.

3.   Lack of height: Although the tension is correct widthways there may be insufficient rows to make the length required.

Action: The hook should sit on top of the work when the loops are being picked up. Frequently the hook is allowed to sit in front of the last row which shortens the loops on the hook, which in turn shortens the work and

makes it a denser fabric using more yarn than necessary.

INCREASING

Before picking up the next vertical strand, which includes the first stitch at the beginning of a row, insert the hook under the horizontal strand lying between the stitch just worked and the next stitch. Collect the yarn in the hook head and pull through onto the hook in the usual way. Continue in simple stitch.

DECREASING

There are different methods of decreasing but the one described here is the least confusing. Decrease on the pick-up row by inserting the hook under two vertical strands at the same time and pulling the yarn through both these strands at once, leaving only one loop for two stitches on the hook. To make decreases look symmetrical within the same piece of fabric, at the end of the row, pick up the two vertical strands before the last one.

JOINING YARN

Whether changing yarn or joining in a new ball, leave sufficient length of the last yarn used to oversew into the loops at the back of the work - then pull the new yarn through, also leaving a length sufficient to oversew in the opposite direction at the back of the work. It is important that the ends are not oversewn on the same row as it will create bulk that can be felt on inspection.

RIGHT SIDE OF TUNISIAN WORK

Unlike the usual form of crochet which has no right or wrong side to it unless you make it have a right or a wrong side, Tunisian crochet is worked with the right side facing you. There are always exceptions to any rules and there are exceptions to this one also but these are not being dealt with in this volume.

The action of having the right side facing during the time of work is advantageous for one handed people as the hook can be placed in a clamp and worked quite quickly with minimum inconvenience.

USING COLOUR

a)   Straight 'clean' stripes are formed when a new colour is joined in at the end of the take-off action, ie at the point where there are only 2 lps left on the hook. Join in the new colour at this point. This avoids a colour drag and makes all the loops on the next pick-up action in the same colour.

b)   The 'Tweed' effect is achieved when the new colour is joined into the work at the point where all the loops have been picked up.

joining in a coloured yarn in Tunisian simple stitch

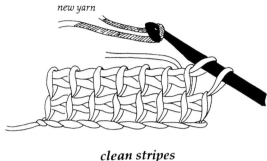

clean stripes

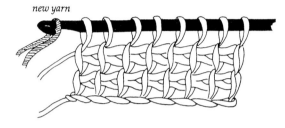

tweed effect

FINISHING OFF TUNISIAN SIMPLE STITCH

Use an ordinary crochet hook two sizes smaller than the size of Tunisian hook being used. Continue to pick up only the vertical strand at the front of the work and make 1dc in every strand to the end. That is pick up in the normal Tunisian simple stitch way but work a full double crochet leaving no loops on the hook. DO NOT GO THROUGH THE WORK.

Tunisian crochet curls whilst being worked. This is to be expected if the work is not being turned. Do not worry. Most patterns will have added edges that will counteract the curling.

Working a double crochet border into the sides of the Tunisian fabric can cause apprehension as one side looks like normal crochet chains which can be worked in double crochet in the usual manner but the other side requires one horizontal AND the single loose strand to be picked up and worked together to make the double crochet stitch.

picking up at edge

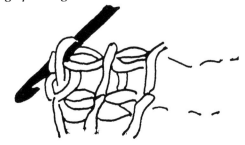

1.   Make a cushion cover in simple stitch incorporating stripes and tweed effects.

2.   Make a cushion cover using the Tunisian treble stitch [described later]

3.   Make a tubular scarf using any of the stitches described in any pattern book. Fold in two lengthways with the right sides together, stitch or crochet to form a tube. Turn inside out and with right sides facing join the two ends together and add some form of decoration such as a fringe.

4.   Using a fashion yarn make 2 matching rectangles leaving sufficient room for the head on one of the short sides. Join the remainder for shoulders. Place this over the head to find where to commence the join for the side seams. Often this design is best left with 5-8cm unjoined at the hem line for vents which gives a better fit.

5.   Make a selection of 15cm squares using a variety of Tunisian stitches and different yarns. Join these together to make a knee rug.

6   Make 2 rectangles using dishcloth cotton of a suitable size for a bag. Work sufficient length on only a few stitches in either Tunisian simple stitch, or double crochet, to go round 2 long sides and one short side.
     Attach to either wooden or crochet handles.

TUNISIAN TREBLE

One chain is required at the start of the row to give the work necessary lift and to stop the sides puckering. Wrap the yarn over the hook once before inserting the hook into the vertical strand, yoh, pull through vertical strand, yoh, pull through 2 loops (do not repeat this process as you would in ordinary crochet or there will be no loops left on the hook for the next process). Continue in this way to the end of the row and remove the loops as for Tunisian simple stitch.

TUNISIAN DOUBLE TREBLE

Make 2ch at start of row and work as for Tunisian treble having wrapped the yarn round the hook twice before inserting it into the work. When removing the loops (yoh, pull through two loops) twice.

JOINING SHOULDER SEAMS INVISIBLY

To join the shoulders or any other seams without it being visible place the right side of one piece of Tunisian to the right side of the other piece of Tunisian fabric before any double crochet has been worked. Each stitch should match exactly with the stitches of the other piece of fabric.

Using a hook that is smaller than the Tunisian hook, work one double crochet through the vertical strand of the fabric nearest you AND the vertical strand of the fabric furthest away from you.

NOTE: It is very important if you start to pick up the loop nearest you first, you always pick up the loop nearest you first.

BUTTONHOLES

To make a buttonhole miss one stitch when picking up the stitches and work one chain when removing the stitches of that row.

Hairpin crochet has copied Sol Lace by making loops that can be gathered together in a variety of ways. To use hairpin creatively it is necessary to make strips of suitable length on a hairpin prong which can then be crocheted together or linked according to preference.

As in Broomstick crochet the size of crochet hook used relates to the thickness of yarn and NOT the width of the prong.

Tips in making Hairpin Lace

1.   It is easier to make the strip a little longer than is required and then pull back a few loops than to have to add loops.

2   Safety pins, tie tackings or knitting markers every 25 loops make counting easier.

3.   When the prong is full and the loops need to be removed for extra length to be added, the strip should be rolled over a piece of card, disused bobbin, or some other item and then hooked onto the base of the prong with a safety pin. This stops the strip twisting and creating an uneven tension.

4.   When joining strips together in groups of more than one loop at a time,   split the number of loops between the base of the first group on the left hand strip and the top of that same strip. This will help the strips to stay levelled at base and at top.

MAKING THE BASIC STRIP

There are different ways to hold both the yarn and the crochet hook in any form of crochet work, therefore other ways to the ones suggested, are not wrong. The most important thing is to make sure that the tension is even, that the work looks neat, and that when the article is finished it will wash and wear well. Similarly, the way you hold the hairpin prong may be different, and this does not matter as long as the finished result is pleasing to look at and suitable for the purpose for which it was designed.

Holding the prong

1   Have the prong shaped like a 'U' with the connecting piece at the bottom

2   Place a slip knot on the crochet hook

3   Hold the yarn in the normal way

4   Place the prong in the hand in such a way that the

yarn attached to the hook comes from behind the prong, round the right hand spoke, to the front

5 Collect the yarn in the hook head and draw through the loop already on the hook. Try to make sure that this loop is now positioned centrally between the two upright spokes of the prong.

6 Turn the prong as the page of a book but first lift the hook into an upright position so that it does not catch on the prong whilst it is being turned.

7 The yarn is automatically wrapped round the righthand spoke, draw the yarn through the loop on the hook

8 Insert the hook under the front strand of the loop at the left and work 1dc round this

making the first loops

a)

b)
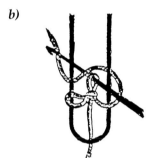

c)
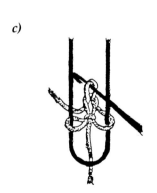

d)
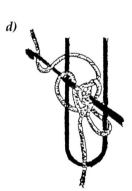

Repeat points 6,7 and 8 until sufficient loops have been made

Alternative method of starting Hairpin:

Make a large loop, slip the loop over both prongs with the tail end of knot in the centre. Twist front loop behind back loop, collect yarn, 1ch, and continue from point 6 above.

alternative starting method

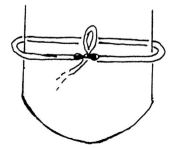

CROCHET SPINE [ie crochet between loops wrapped round 2 spokes]

Unless told otherwise it is usual for the centre of a hairpin spine to be 1dc in the front loop on the left hand side

Broader and different styles of spine can be made by substituting the 1dc for any of the following:

1 2dc in front loop of lefthand side
2 1ch1dc in front loop of lefthand side
3 1tr in front loop of lefthand side
4 2tr in front loop of lefthand side
5 1tr 1htr 1dc in front loop of lefthand side
6 3ch 1ss in first ch, 1dc in front loop of lefthand side
7 To open up the loops so that they are flatter and more elastic, work into the back loop of the lefthand side.

There are many more variations and it is an interesting experiment to 'play' with various stitch combinations in the centre of the hairpin strip.

All the above variations are worked with the spine of crochet in the centre of the hairpin strip. The crochet can be worked 'off-centre' and the patterns given here are suitable for household linen, lampshades, edges of stoles, shawls, etc.

HAIRPIN FRINGE - looped

Use a large prong between 60 and 100mm and a 5 or 8 mercerised cotton. Acrylic crepe and any other yarn can be used if it is not being subjected to heat, strong light and exposed to dusty atmospheres. Alternatively use 2-4 finer threads together and work them as one yarn.

Position the working of the crochet as close to a working spoke as possible. Work a length of hairpin crochet keeping the spine in a straight line close to the prong, sufficiently long to go round a lampshade, stool, shawl etc. For household items the fringe should be slightly stretched as it is placed on the article. With fashion items the fringe should be eased fractionally so that there is no pulling if the fabric stretches.

The long loops can be cut if desired. This is most effective if a group of threads has been used as one yarn.

The short loops require an edge to hold the loops firmly in position and should have a picot, crab stitch, or other decorative last row over the slip stitches or double crochet stitches used to give the correct size to the top edge. The distance between the edge and the spine can be filled with some kind of surface crochet such as tambour chains etc. Whatever is produced from the spine to the edge can then be repeated as a braid for the top edge of a lampshade.

CROCHET BRAID

This is a piece of hairpin worked centrally with a 20mm or 30mm prong using very thick yarn. Work a spine that will fill the space between the spokes of the prong completely. When sufficient length has been obtained work an edging on both sides, using the loops from the spokes. Remember a braid should have an interesting finish on both sides or it stops being a braid and becomes an edging.

JOINS

There are many different ways to join strips of hairpin together, not all of them requiring a crochet hook and extra yarn.

Joining by linking

When linking two strips of hairpin together it is better to be at a table for the first attempt so that the two strips can lie side by side without twisting. Insert the hook through the bottom loop of the left-hand strip on the right side of the crochet. * Pull the bottom two loops of the RH strip through the two loops on the hook, pull the next two loops on the RH strip through the two loops on the hook. Rep from * until the two strips have been joined. You should end with one loop on the RH side. Leave this loop in a safety pin until such time as an edging or finishing row is added to the work.

NOTE: the number of loops you pull through each other will depend upon how you want the fabric to look and also on the thickness of the yarn to the width of the prong. Experiment with different numbers of loop connections before working the whole into an article. Remember to divide the number of chosen loops into two for the first grouping from a strip so that the base line and the top line will be level.

linking strips

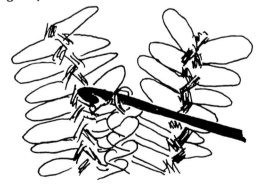

Faggot join

Decide how many loops are to be collected in a group before commencing. Join the yarn to half that number on one of the strips, *3ch, 1dc in group of loops of next strip, 3ch, 1dc in next group of loops in first strip, rep from * to end with the last dc being working into half the number of loops of a group.

faggot join

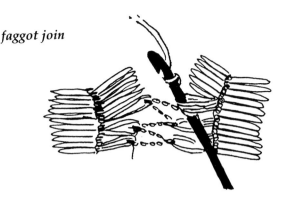

The pattern below for a curtain incorporates a number of different joins including one that changes the straight line of the spine into curves.

CURTAIN

Materials: 6 balls No.10 mercerized cotton: 30mm and 80mm hiarpin prongs: 1.75mm crochet hook: small beads for adding weight to the curtain if desired.

Size: The instructions are given for a curtain that measures 65cm deep x 80cm wide [25 x 31.5in] Add approximately 6 loops each side for every 5cm [2in] extra width and add further strips of hairpin alternating the 30mm and 80mm hairpin prongs for length.

Tension: All hairpin crochet is difficult to measure exactly tension-wise on stitches. The overall length of the strips of hairpin with equal numbers of loops on each strip for the joining, are the most important factors.

TO MAKE

Using a basic central spine of 1dc under front loop, work 5 strips of hairpin on the 30mm hairpin prong with 240 loops on each side.

Using the same basic spine, work 7 strips of hairpin on the 80mm prong with 240 loops on each side.

Joining the Strips

Following the figure below work as follows

Step 1: Join cotton through 2 loops of strip A and 2 loops of B, 1ch to act as a dc, continue working through 2 loops from each strip tog *1ch, 1dc through 4 loops rep from * to end.
Step 2: Join B to C by linking 2 loops of C through 2 loops of B.
Step 3: Join C to D as in Step 1
Step 4: Join D to E by linking
Step 5: Join E to F as in Step 1
Step 6: Join F to G by linking
Step 7: Join G to H as in Step 1
Should the curtain need to be longer, lengthen it here by repeating the last two steps
Step 8: Join H to I (2 narrow strips) by linking
Step 9: Put the first 6 loops of strip J into a safety pin, *leave 12 loops free, group 12 loops in a saftey pin, rep

from * to end placing last 6 loops in a pin. Join yarn to 3 loops of strip I, 3ch, 1dc in first 6 loops of J, *(3ch, 1dc in 3 loops of I, 1dc in 2 loops of J)6 times, 3ch, 1dc in 3 loops of I, 3ch, 1dc in 12 loops of J, rep from * to end connecting the last 6 loops of J.

Step 10: On J leave 6 loops, *place 12 loops in pin, leave 12 loops, rep from * to end having 6 loops free. Collect the loops for strip K exactly as the first side of strip J. Join cotton to first group of 6 loops on K, *2ch 1dc in a group on J, 2ch 1dc in a group on K [this will be either a group of 2 or a group of 12].

NOTE SPECIALLY: the 12 group loops should be exactly under each other.

Step 11: Join K to L as in step 10

Step 12: Thread beads onto cotton. Divide loops of L into groups of 12 as though an extra strip was to be added. Join the yarn to 2 loops, 3ch, 1dc in next group of loops all along the row placing a bead or beads in the centre of the curve when that point is reached.

Heading

Join yarn to 5 loops of strip A, *4ch, 1dc in next 5 loops, rep from * to end, 1ch, turn.

Row 2: *4dc in 4chsp, 1dc in dc, rep from * to end.
Fasten off.
A rod can be threaded through the spaces just made to hang the curtain.

position of strips for curtain

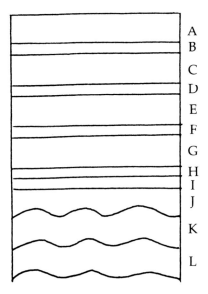

CHAPTER TEN
FILET CROCHET

ORIGINS

The name 'filet crochet' is a term handed down from early to mid-19th century at a time when crochet began to copy the patterns of laces. Filet lace is a very smooth lace worked with a needle. The crochet copy of filet designs produces ridges on each row unlike the real filet lace which has nothing to give it contrast or shadows.

One reason for the popularity of crochet in the style of filet lace is the ease with which it can be charted on graph paper using a cross for a block and leaving the square blank for a space. This makes it relatively simple to create geometric designs, lace with the written word included, and all manner of shapes which portray a theme. In addition a simple sketch or photograph showing the completed item, made it possible for the crochet worker to copy the picture and fully ignore any written instructions or graphed designs. For instance the piece of filet on the inside back cover could be easily reproduced without a pattern.

STITCHES USED

Two stitches only are used in the simple squared network of filet crochet and those are a chain and a treble. These two stitches are then put together to form either a block or a space

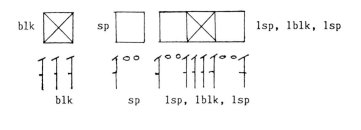

| Block (blk) | = | 3trebles (trs) per square |
| Space (sp) | = | 2chains 1treble (2ch 1tr) per square |

Trebles are worked in the usual way when crocheted on top of trebles. That is pick up the two strands that look like an embroidered chain, at the top of the stitch. However, if the trebles are worked in a space, the first two trebles are usually worked directly into the space under the chain for speed. Depending upon how accurate the trebles have to lie in the piece of filet crochet being worked, this is quite satisfactory. There are just one or two occasions when it is prudent to work the trebles directly into each chain of the space.

Bar and Lacet

The square network is the usual background mesh in filet crochet and is made by the use of spaces (ie 2ch 1tr with each tr sitting on top of the tr below).

The bar and lacet uses two squares on the chart with the lacet looking like the top of an arch and the bar being unmarked.

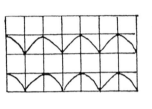 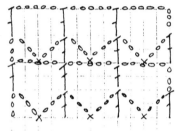

A bar = 5ch 1tr (over 6 stitches ie 2 squares)
A lacet = 3ch, 1dc under the bar (ie the 5ch sp), 3ch, 1tr on tr.

To Calculate chains to commence filet

Using the chart below as a practical example, calculate the number of chains required in the foundation chain as follows:-

	Example		Number
Multiply the number of squares in the chart by 3	6 x 3	=	18
Add 1 for turning	1	=	1
Add 2 if starting with a blk	2	=	2
			21
If starting with a sp add another 2	2	=	23

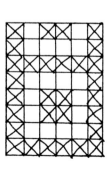 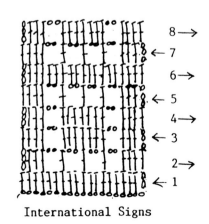

Chart   International Signs

USES OF FILET CROCHET

Household

As with most types of crochet there are no limits to its use. The effectiveness of filet relies on the pattern being produced showing up clearly. This is probably why it is so suitable for household linen which is then placed over tables, chairs, trays, plates etc.

Fashion

Whether cotton or mixed fibres in a smooth yarn are used is of no consequence as both can create interesting designs. The textured fashion yarns can however, detract from the pattern and from the effect being aimed for. This does not apply in all cases but it is important to check on a tension piece that the effect being produced is what you are looking for, before working a whole filet design in a textured yarn.

Choice of materials to hooks

The size of the hook depends upon the thickness of the crochet cotton being worked and the purpose to which the fabric is to be used. Again there are no hard and fast rules, but if household linen is being made the following table may help.

Thickness of Mercerised cotton	Hook size
100's	0.60
80's	0.60-0.75
70,s & 60's	0.60-1.00
40's	0.75-1.25
20's	1.00-1.75
10's	1.25-2.00
5's & 8's	1.50-2.50

The choice of hook size is different for fashion items even if the same yarn is being used. A firm crisp finish is often desirable in household items and therefore a smaller hook is required. In fashion filet crochet a soft fabric is required which means larger hooks are necessary.

INSERTION STRIPS

Insertion strips are usually placed in a non-crochet fabric but can be used to add interest in a plain double crochet, treble or similar fabric. An insertion strip is rather like a braid with both sides the same; in this instance very smooth and plain.

EDGINGS

The difference between an insertion and an edging is an edging usually has only one straight edge, unlike the insertion strip with two straight edges. Filet edgings can be castellated, scalloped or in a Van Dyke (ie chevron) shape. See sketch below

shapes of filet edgings

a) Van Dyke is very pointed chevron

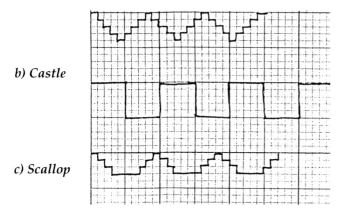

b) Castle

c) Scallop

WHERE TO FIND PATTERNS

Filet is a traditional way of working crochet and as such there are many patterns available dating back to the 1840's. DO look around and find interesting designs other than those in the present day, easily available, books. Museums usually have a library and books in museums are quite a treasure trove.

To finish your work with an added design feature it is possible to make your own buttons and trim the item [where applicable] with a crochet braid. Crocheted buttons and braids can be used on any household or fashion item constructed in any textile!

BUTTONS

It is often not possible for a button of the exact size and colour to be found to suit the needs of a garment. Buttons, however can be made quite quickly and easily.

The points listed below have been found to be helpful to a large number of people and it may be a good idea to read these, before making any button.

* Use a smaller (maybe much smaller) hook than the one used for the main crochet item. This makes the crochet firmer which is an advantage in a button.

* If the yarn used for the article is thick, it can be divided so that only one or two of the plied strands are used.

* If old manufactured buttons are being inserted to make a firm crocheted button, and if the colour of the button shows through the crochet, a small piece of matching material (or even strands of the   yarn itself) can be glued to the surface of the button.

* If the button is to be a soft one and requires filling, avoid cotton wool as it seems to take forever to dry out after laundering! Also avoid foam chips as these do not hold a shape very well and unless a 'nutty' or 'knobbly' effect is required, they are very difficult to handle. Polyester toy filling is quite successful, but like the hard buttons above, the colour may show through.   Should you have enough yarn, a filling made of the yarn itself is by far the best as it is both the right shade and there are no laundry problems involved.

* When using a bead or a button without a shank, the holes in the bead or button can be used for extra security if a sewing stitch worked with an invisible sewing thread is made through the holes. Alternatively use this on a plain style button for added design interest.

* Remember that a crocheted buttonhole is often quite thick, so the button being attached to the buttonband may require some form of shank. Gathering part of the back of a button can be an advantage.

* Mark the position of the buttons before making the buttonholes and then be absolutely positive that the button matches the buttonhole exactly after it has been sewn to the garment.   Puckered seams and irregularly

unplanned buttons/buttonholes make beautiful work look home-made and unprofessional.

Buttons come in different groupings and the pattern of an example of one style is given in three of the groups. There are no hook sizes given as all the patterns can be made in any yarn. The hook selection should be made after looking at the points given above.

The neatest buttons are those made directly into the slip knot BUT the slip knot must draw up into a tighter loop from the short end of the yarn and not the ball end.

soft centres

These are the kind filled with their own yarn or polyester fibre, etc.

Simple 'Pierrot' style

Rnd 1: 3ch, 11tr in slip knot, join with ss to top of 3ch.
Rnd 2: 1ch, 1dc in each tr, ss to beg of rnd
Rnd 3: As rnd 2

Leave a 20cm end of yarn and darn this end through the top of the last row. Before closing the gap, fill the centre. Draw the yarn up tightly and fasten off securely.

hard centres

flat button   *bead centre*   *mouldwith shank*

The button described above can be used to insert a button mould, bead, or old button. It is important to remember that crochet stretches so a tight-fitting button cover is needed for a successful finish.

Button to take a hard flat button with shank

2ch, 8dc in slip knot, do not join
2htr in each dc to end

Thread a 20cm yarn through each stitch
Stretch cover over the mould or button and draw up firmly before finishing off. Use the shank of the button inside the crochet cover to attach the to article.

unfilled buttons

It is possible to make buttons without any additional filling but in such instances it is <u>very important</u> that a small hook for the thickness of yarn, is selected. Unfilled buttons are ideal in areas where the button is more of a design feature than a utility commodity.

Firm Flat Button

Rnd 1: 2ch, 7htr in slip knot, ss to top of ch.
Rnd 2: Crab st in front loop only of each htr.
Rnd 3: 1ch, 2dc in back loops of each htr [behind the crab st], ss to join.
Rnd 4: Crab st in front loop of each dc, ss to join
Rnd 5: 1ch, dc to end (16 sts)
Rnd 6: 1ch, *1dc, dc2tog, rep from * to end, ss to join (10sts)
Rnd 7: *dc2tog, rep from * to end.
Gather the rem 5 sts tog and secure to article.

There are two other groups of buttons not dealt with here:
Buttons with two or more colours
Flower buttons.

BRAIDS

What is or is not a braid is a debatable point. My <u>personal</u> opinion of a braid is one that is firm, has both edges similar if not identical, and can be applied to other fabrics as an appliquéd accessory.

Use of braids

* Applied as a trim to a tailored suit, dress, collar or other garment
* Used as a binding to neaten edges of woven fabrics
* As insertions into any household or fashion item.

<u>Points to note</u>

* The size of the hook depends on whether the braid required needs to be very firm as in the case of an